YD65

K2

CHALLENGING THE SKY

THE
MOUNTAINEERS

SEATTLE, WASHINGTON

CONTENTS

Text
Roberto Mantovani
and Kurt Diemberger

Editorial production
Valeria Manferto
Laura Accomazzo

Graphic design
Patrizia Balocco Lovisetti

Translation
Neil Davenport

The Publisher would like to thank: Stefano Ardito, Anna Balbiano, Goretta Traverso Casarotto and Manuel Lugli for their valuable assistance.

Special thanks to Istituto Geografico Militare, to Fondazione Sella and the Museo Nazionale della Montagna "Duca degli Abruzzi."

The publisher will fulfill its obligations toward any owners of photographic copyright unable to be traced

This edition published in 1997 by

 The Mountaineers
1001 SW Klickitat Way
Seattle, WA 98134

Produced by: White Star S.r.l.
Via Candido Sassone, 22/24
13100 Vercelli, Italy.

ISBN: 0-89886-518-2

Printed in the month of March 1997 by Conti, Florence (Italy).

10 9 8 7 6 5 4 3 2 1

1 *The last rays of sunlight illuminate K2's elegant pyramid.*
Photograph by Galen Rowell/Mountain Light

2-3 *A pallid moon hangs alongside the imposing bulk of the North Face of the world's second highest mountain.*
Photograph by Pierre Beghin

4-5 *The long line of porters employed by the 1975 American expedition, no less than 650, winding its way up the lower slopes of the Karakoram giant.*
Photograph by Galen Rowell/Mountain Light

6-7 *Members of the 1978 American expedition tackling the snowy slopes of K2. The snow was so deep that the climbers sank to their waists and advancing just a few metres was exhausting.*
Photograph by John Roskelley

8 *The summit of K2 shrouded in its characteristic cap of clouds.*
Photograph by Galen Rowell/Mountain Light

9 *Two climbing teams from the 1978 American expedition led by Jim Whittaker crossing a tricky section of crest. In these situations the climber must be extremely careful not to climb too close to the peak of the ice rib, as his weight might cause the unstable snow to collapse.*
Photograph by John Roskelley

10-11 *The delicate snow formations and a glacier protruding from the steep slopes adorn the harsh, severe walls of K2's North Face.*
Photograph by Greg Child

12-13 *Greg Mortimer, a member of the American-Australian expedition to the North Ridge in 1990, sinking into the deep snow close to camp II.*
Photograph by Greg Child

A DREAM FACTORY

*E*ight thousand six hundred and sixteen metres of rock, snow and ice rising out of an area of geological chaos. A vast pyramid, the largest and highest on earth. A mysterious, hidden world. One so inaccessible that a gruelling trek is the price to be paid for a glimpse of the slopes of K2. That said, distance and inaccessibility have never constituted insurmountable obstacles for dedicated mountaineers. For over a century now the massive K2, the true keystone to the great Karakoram Range, has played a leading role in the history of Himalayan climbing. This mountain has exerted a magnetic attraction over generations of climbers. It has stimulated the formation of immense caravans of men, involved climbers in desperate struggles and provided extraordinary adventures, and it has also been responsible for great tragedies. "These are mountains which you cannot observe without being moved; mountains which seem to embrace fearful mysteries" wrote Filippo De Filippi, the diarist on the Duke of the Abruzzi's expedition early this century. He was not wrong. There is an indefinable atmosphere about K2, something strange which has to be experienced directly, face to face.

The great rocky pyramid has none of the softness of the Nepalese mountains. Rather than a green valley, the mountain overlooks great rivers of ice and a forest of peaks of varying height, many still unnamed. In the evening its majestic shadow extends over the seracs of the Godwin Austen Glacier and the icy slopes of Broad Peak's north summit. K2 is domineering, charged with an unusual, insistently vibrating energy. There is nothing idyllic or restful in its beauty.

It is a hard, jagged landscape with a subtly disturbing appeal for onlookers. It is a magnificent, unforgiving peak, undoubtedly more masculine than feminine. But above all it represents a prelude to infinity, a promise of the absolute. A mute, almost arcane message. Massive, yet perfect, regular and dynamic in form, the giant of the Karakoram Range is a mountain of many faces, each one unique.

Over 3,500 metres high, the concave, tortuous South Face was the first to be admired by the early pioneers, and the first to be known in Europe thanks to the superb photographs taken by Vittorio Sella during the Duke of the Abruzzi's

expedition of 1909. The classic K2 images, taken from the South, have a familiar air about them. They are undoubtedly those most frequently published, but there is more to it than that. "There is no need for words to demonstrate the great similarity between K2 seen from the South and the Matterhorn," wrote Filippo De Filippi in 1912. And we have to agree. The great South Face is slashed obliquely by a glacier tumbling from the East Shoulder, 900 metres below the summit, with four cascades of seracs. At the Eastern end of the South Face, the Abruzzi Ridge rises out of the Godwin Austen Glacier directly to the summit of the Shoulder. From the opposite side of the face, another great rocky rib, the South-South-West Ridge, climbs 2,300 metres from the notch forming the Negrotto Saddle, to the summit, and represents some of the most grandiose and beautiful of K2's natural architecture.

Then comes the immense Western Face. Endless rock with great hanging glaciers and serried seracs. The South-West Ridge extends for over four kilometres, while the North-West Ridge rises from the base of the Savoia Glacier at the saddle of the same name. Moving farther round, into the Sinkiang region, we find the Northern Flank, the monstrous white wall which in 1937 enchanted the English explorer Eric Shipton. First there is the almost all-rock North-West Face, then the immense North Ridge with a linear development of almost four kilometres. Then there is the incredibly high North Face, incised by a deep vertical channel overlooked by a hanging glacier which tops out at 7,300 metres. The long North-East Ridge, "an uninterrupted precipitous wall, all ice and perpendicular rocky ribs," straddles the border between China and Pakistan.

Our circumnavigation of this pyramid is completed by the snow and ice covered Eastern Flank. This could almost be another mountain, the "extreme cone" of which, recalled De Filippi, "rises from a great inclined shoulder, entirely covered by a glacier which descends to its brow and breaks off suddenly to form a perennial threat to all the channels, furrows and ridges of the steep slope below." The reality of K2 proved capable of transforming the collective imagination of an era.

15 *The passage of the sun over the different faces of K2 — this shot is of the North Face — offers spectacular photo opportunities. Photograph by F. Marsigny/ Agence Freestyle*

16-17 *The summit of K2 is frequently shrouded in dense clouds which hide it from view, but as soon as they lift the sight is truly spectacular. Photograph by Greg Child*

18-19 *This map of the Baltoro Glacier was drawn up on the basis of surveys made during the 1929 and 1954 expeditions. (Map negatives courtesy Military Geographical Institute. Authorisation No. 4212 of 31.05.1995.)*

GHIACCIAIO

a Carta al 75000 della spedizione geografica Italiana (1929)

b Carta al 12500 della spedizione Italiana al K2 (1954)

c Rilievo stereofotogrammetrico terrestre della spedizione Italiana (1954)

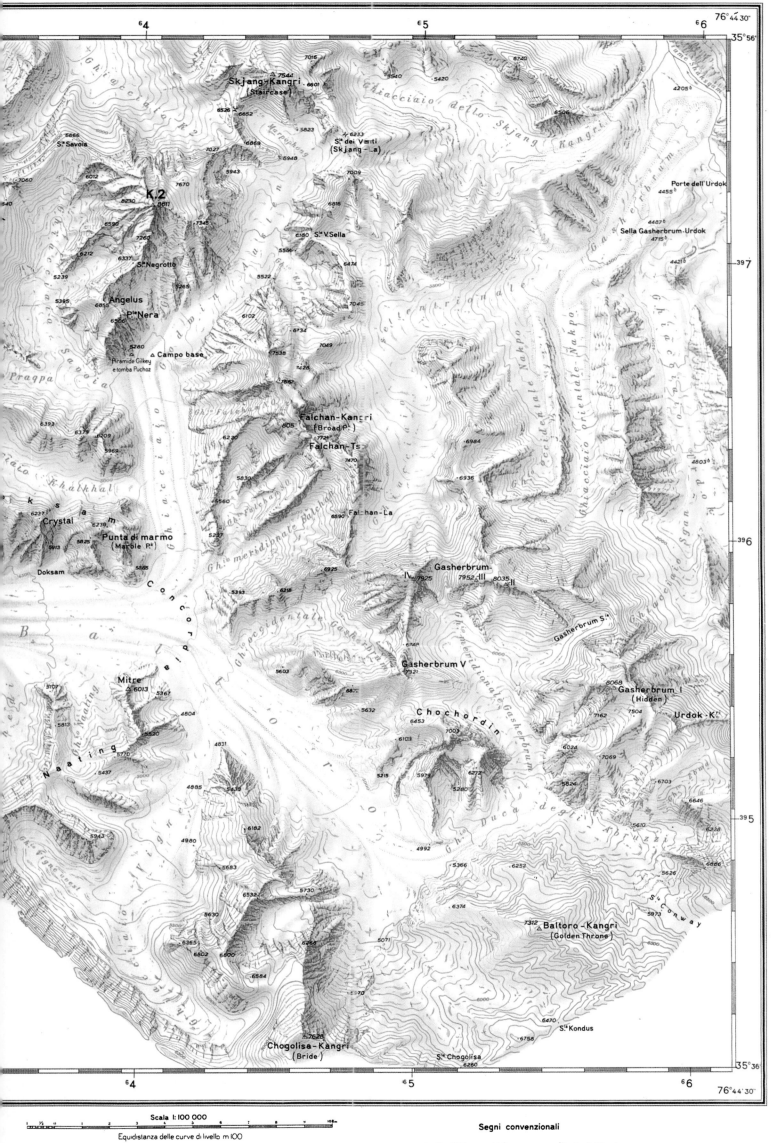

1977: A Japanese expedition led by Ichiro Yoshizawa. The second ascent of K2 along the Abruzzi Ridge. On the 8th and 9th of August seven climbers, six Japanese and one Pakistani, reached the summit with the aid of oxygen.

1978: A British expedition along the South-West Ridge led by Chris Bonington. The attempt was called off following the death of Nick Estcourt, buried by an avalanche below camp II.

1978: The third successful ascent, this time by an American expedition led by Jim Whittaker. The climbers followed the 1976 Polish route up to 7,700 metres, and then continued along the Abruzzi Ridge. Four climbers reached the summit on the 6th and 7th of September.

1979: An international expedition under the leadership of Reinhold Messner. The "Magic Line" project was abandoned and the climbers followed the Abruzzi Ridge. On the 12th of June Messner and Michl Dacher reached the summit (fourth ascent).

1979: A French expedition led by Bernard Mellet. The attempt on the South-South-West Ridge reached 8,350 metres.

1980: A British expedition under Chris Bonington. An attempt on the West Ridge reached 7,000 metres, while another along the Abruzzi Ridge reached 8,000 metres.

22 top *The American route, 1978, the North-East Ridge, East Face, Abruzzi Ridge.*
Photograph by Rollo Steffens

22 centre *Japanese route, 1981.*
Photograph by Ramon Portilla

22 bottom *North Face, Japanese route, 1982.*
Photograph by Ramon Portilla

1960: A German-American expedition led by Major William Hackett. The climbers were forced to turn back by bad weather at 7,260 metres.

1975: An American expedition led by Jim Whittaker. An attempt was made on the North-West Ridge which reached 6,700 metres.

1976: A Polish expedition directed by Janusz Kurczab. The group attempted the North-East Ridge (see 1902) and reached 8,400 metres. Oxygen was used only above 8,000 metres.

1981: A Japanese attempt on the South-West Ridge led by Teruo Matsuura. This was the fifth successful climb and established a new route. Eiho Otani and Nazir Sabir reached the peak on the 7th of August.

1981: A Franco-German expedition led by Yannick Seigneur. An attempt was made on the South Face which reached 7,400 metres.

1982: A Polish expedition led by Janusz Kurczab tackled the North-West Ridge. The climbers reached 8,200 metres before being forced back by bad weather.

23 *A climber from the American expedition led by Jim Whittaker (1978) climbing a steep, snow-covered slope on K2. Photograph by John Roskelley*

1982: A Japanese expedition led by Isao Shinkai and Masatsugu Konishi. This was the sixth ascent of K2 and the first ascent via the Northern Flank. On the 14th and 15th of August no less than seven climbers reached the summit of K2, all without oxygen: Naoè Sakashita, Yukihiro Yanagisawa, Hiroshi Yoshino, Kazushige Takami, Haruischi Kawamura, Tatsuji Shigeno and Hironobu Kamuro. Yanagisawa died during the descent.

1982: An Austrian expedition directed by Hanns Schell. The group reached 7,350 metres before going to the aid of the Polish expedition bringing down the body of a climber who died at camp II.

1982: A female Polish expedition led by Wanda Rutkiewicz. An attempt was made along the Abruzzi Ridge. Halina Krüger-Syrokomska died of a heart attack at camp II.

1983: A Spanish expedition led by Antonio Trabado attempted the West Face. The climbers reached 8,200 metres.

1983: An international expedition under the leadership of Doug Scott. The attempt to open up a new route on the South Face, to the left of the Abruzzi Ridge, ended at 7,600 metres.

1983: A Spanish expedition led by Gregorio Ariz. Following the withdrawal of the main expedition, Mari Abrego and the Englishman Roger Baxter Jones (a member of the Scott expedition) pushed on to 8,300 metres along the usual route.

1987: A Swiss-Polish expedition led by Wojciech Kurtyka to the West Face. The climbers reached only 6,400 metres.

1987: A Japanese expedition led by Haruyuki Endo along the Abruzzi Ridge. The attempt was abandoned at 7,400 metres.

1987: A Japanese-Pakistani expedition led by Kenshiro Otaki along the Abruzzi Ridge. The climbers reached 8,300 metres before being forced back. Akiro Suzuki died during the descent.

1987: A Basque expedition directed by Juanjo San Sebastián attempted the South-South-East Ridge and then the usual route. The climbers reached 8,350 metres.

1987-88: A Polish winter expedition led by Andrzej Zawada along the Abruzzi Ridge. The attempt was abandoned at 7,350 metres.

1988: A Yugoslavian expedition led by Tomas Jamnik along the South-South-West Ridge. The attempt failed at 8,100 metres, and subsequently the climbers attacked the Abruzzi Ridge but were forced back at 7,400 metres.

1988: An American expedition led by Peter Athans along the Abruzzi Ridge. The climbers reached 7,400 metres.

1988: A New Zealand expedition led by Robert Hall attempted the Abruzzi Ridge. Again the climbers were forced back at 7,400 metres.

1988: A Spanish-Catalan attempt on the Abruzzi Ridge led by Jordi Magriñá reached 8,100 metres.

1988: A French expedition led by Pierre Beghin along the North Ridge. The climb ended at 8,000 metres.

1989: A Swiss-Polish expedition led by Wojciech Kurtyka attempted the North-West Face. The attempt failed due to bad weather

1989: An Austrian expedition led by Eduard Koblmüller on the virgin East Face. Hans Bärnthaler died on the 27th of July.

1989: A Basque expedition led by Juanjo San Sebastián along the Abruzzi Ridge. The climbers were forced back at 7,400 metres.

1990: An American expedition led by Doug Dalcuist along the Abruzzi Ridge. The climbers reached 7,000 metres.

1990: The "Free K2" Mountain Wilderness international expedition led by Carlo Alberto Pinelli. The group cleared much of the Abruzzi Ridge of fixed ropes and the abandoned remains of the high altitude camps.

1990: A Japanese expedition led by Tomaji Ueki. On the 9th of August Hideji Nazuka and Hirotaka Imamura reached the summit after climbing a route along the North-West Face as far as 7 000 metres and then continuing along the 1982 Japanese route.

1990: An American-Australian expedition directed by Steve Swenson. The goal was that of repeating the Japanese 1982 climb. On the 20th of August Greg Child, Greg Mortimer and Steve Swenson reached the summit.

1991: A German party led by Sigi Hupfauer climbed the Abruzzi Ridge as far as the Shoulder.

1991: An Italian expedition led by Fabio Agostinis attempted to establish a new route along the North-West Face. The attempt was abandoned at 8,200 metres.

26 Greg Mortimer and Phil Ershler climbing the canal which begins at camp III on the North Face of K2. Here the altitude is around 7,600 metres. On the 20th of August, 1990, after having repeated the Japanese route, Greg Mortimer, Greg Child and Steve Swenson reached the summit.
Photograph by Greg Child

27 The Japanese route, 1990.
Photograph by Ramon Portilla

1991: The French climbers Pierre Beghin and Christophe Profit followed the North-West Ridge, diagonally traversed the North-West Face and finally followed the 1982 Japanese route. They reached the summit on the 15th of August.

1991: The New Zealanders Robert Hall and Gary Ball climbed the Abruzzi Ridge, but were forced back at 7,600 metres.

1992: The Pole Wojciech Kurtyka and the Swiss Erhard Loretan attempted a new route on the West Face but turned back after reaching 6,400 metres; the constant danger of avalanches forced the climb to be abandoned.

1992: A large international expedition led by the Russian climber Vladimir Balyberdin on the Abruzzi Ridge. On the 1st of August Balyberdin and Gennady Kopieka reached the summit, followed by the Ukrainian Aleksei Nikiforov on the 3rd and the Americans Ed Viesturs, Scott Fischer and Charley Mace on the 16th.

1992: A Swiss-French group led by Peter Schwitter attempted the Abruzzi Ridge but turned back after reaching 7,600 metres. Subsequently the French Alpinist Chantal Mauduit joined the Balyberdin expedition and reached the summit of K2 on the 3rd of August.

1992: An international expedition led by the Mexican Ricardo Torres climbed the Abruzzi Ridge but was forced back at 8,000 metres, shortly after the death of Adrián Benítez.

1993: An international expedition led by the Slovenian Tomaz Jamnik reached the summit via the usual Abruzzi Ridge route. The Mexican Carlos Carsolio, the Croatian Stipe Bozic and the Slovenians Viki Groselj and Zvonko Pozgaj reached the top of K2 on the 13th of June. Bostjan Kekec died while attempting to reach the summit. Lastly, the Swede Göran Kropp also reached the top on the 23rd of June.

1993: An American expedition led by Stacy Allison was concluded on the 7th of July with three climbers reaching the summit: the American Phil Powers, and the Canadians Jim Haberl and Dan Culver. The latter fell to his death during the descent.

1993: An international team led by the German climber Reinmar Joswig followed the usual K2 ascent route. Joswig, the Kazakstani Anatoli Bukreev, the German Peter Mezger and the Australian Andrew Lock reached the summit on the 30th of July. Mezger and Joswig fell to their deaths during the descent.

1993: A Swedish expedition captained by Magnus Nilsson climbed the Abruzzi Ridge. On the 30th of July Rafael Jensen and Daniel Bindner reached the summit together with other climbers from the Joswig expedition. During the descent Bindner began to suffer from the symptoms of cerebral edema, lost his balance and fell.

1993: A British expedition led by Roger Payne attempted the Abruzzi Ridge but turned back after going to the aid of the Swede Rafael Jensen.

1993: A Basque group led by Félix Iñurrategi attempted the North Ridge but was forced back after reaching 8,000 metres.

1993: An international expedition led by the Russian Vladimir Balyberdin attempted the North Ridge but only got as high as 6,800 metres.

1993: A Canadian expedition led by Peter Arbic attempted to repeat the South-South-West route but was forced back 400 metres above the Negrotto Saddle. Subsequently the climbers attempted the Kukuczka-Piotrowski route and, from a height of 6,000 metres, moved to the South-South-East Ridge. Having reached the Shoulder they followed the usual route up to 8,000 metres before returning to the base camp.

28 The French route, Beghin-Profit, 1991. Photograph by Ramon Portilla

29 Christophe Profit leading the team through a passage on the new route which in part follows the North-West Face of K2. Photograph by Pierre Beghin

1993: An international team led by Wim Van Harskamp attempted the Abruzzi Ridge; the climbers turned back after reaching 7,400 metres.

1993: A Spanish expedition led by Josep Aced attempted the Cesen route, reaching 7,200 metres.

1993: An international party led by the Englishman Jonathan Pratt and the American Dan Mazur made the second ascent of the South-West Ridge; they reached the summit on the 2nd of September.

1994: A Basque group led by Juan Oiarzabal climbed the South-South-East Ridge and then proceeded along the classic route to the summit. On the 23rd of June Oiarzabal, Alberto and Félix Iñurrategi, De Pablo and Tomáz reached the top.

1994: A Polish-American group composed of Kurtyka, Wielicki and Buhler followed the Cesen route, but had to turn back before reaching the top.

1994: A commercial expedition led by Dujmovits offered to take climbers of various nationalities to the summit. On the 9th of July the New Zealander Hall reached the summit; on the 23rd the exploit was repeated by the leader, the Finn Gustafsson and the Germans Schlönvogt and Wärthl.

1994: An international team led by David Bridges attempted the Abruzzi Ridge. On the 23rd of July the Australian Mike Groom reached the summit.

1994: A Ukrainian group led by Sviridenko attempted the classic route along the Abruzzi Ridge. Three climbers died on the 11th of July: Ibragimzade, Parkhomenko and Kharaldin. On the 23rd Benko and Mstislev reached the summit.

1994: A Spanish expedition directed by Angel Rifa climbed as far as 300 metres above camp II on the Abruzzi Ridge.

1994: A team of Korean climbers led by Kim-In-Tae reached camp III on the Abruzzi Ridge.

1994: A Japanese group led by Kinoshi abandoned an attempt on the Abruzzi Ridge a short way below camp II.

1994: The Japanese expedition directed by Sakamara withdrew shortly before establishing camp IV close to the Shoulder of K2. The group attempted the classic route.

1994: An Anglo-American team composed of the brothers Alan and Adrian Burgess, Alan Hinkes, Brad Johnson, Paul Moores and Mark Wilford attempted a repeat climb of the North Ridge. Hinkes reached a height of 8,100 metres.

1994: A Basque expedition led by Tamayo attacked the North Ridge. On the 30th of July Tamayo and De La Cruz reached the summit. They were followed by San Sebastián and Apellániz on the 4th of August. Following a demanding bivouac at a height of 8,500 metres, Apellániz died of cerebral edema during the descent.

1994: An Italian expedition led by Don Arturo Bergamaschi attempted to open up a new route on the North-West Face. Before turning back, the lead climbers reached 8,450 metres.

1995: The first news of the summer. On the 17th of July the Dutchmen Ronald Naar and Hans Van der Meulen, the Briton Alan Hinkes and the Sherpas Rajab and Norba Shah reached the summit via the Abruzzi Ridge. On the 12th of August, Alison Hargreaves and Rob Slater, a New Zealand expedition led by Peter Hillary (all of them following the Abruzzi Ridge), as well as a Spanish team along the South-South-East Ridge, reached camp IV. On the 13th, Olivar, Escartin, Ortiz, Grant, Hargreaves and Slater made an attempt on the summit. The others withdrew (Lakes was to die of pulmonary edema at camp II). In the afternoon, Ortiz and Grant, Hargreaves and Olivar reached the top separately (did Escartin and Slater make the final climb?). At dusk the six climbers disappeared in bad weather.

30 *The Cesen route, 1986 and the Abruzzi Ridge, 1994.*
Photograph by Ramon Portilla

30-31 *Summer 1994: the Italian expedition led by Don Arturo Bergamaschi attempted to open up a new route along the North-West Wall of K2. The climbers were, however, forced to turn back just 150 metres from the summit.*
Photograph by Manuel Lugli

By the 15th of August 1995, 122 climbers had reached the summit of K2, relatively few considering the number of expeditions which have attempted the climb since 1902.

Eighty of the successful climbers reached the top via the Abruzzi Ridge, four by first climbing the North-East Ridge and then the Abruzzi Ridge; four via the South-West Ridge; 20 climbed the North Ridge; two via the South Face; three climbed the South-South-West Ridge; two reached the top via the crest and the North-West Face and then the North Face; finally seven climbers made it to the summit via the South-South-East Ridge.

The death toll is tragically high: 45 climbers have lost their lives on the slopes of K2.

take a look at K2. This was not easy as the giant of the Karakoram Range is invisible from the middle of the Baltoro, its great bulk being hidden by high rocky buttresses. Godwin Austen was not easily deterred, however, and climbed in the direction of Masherbrum until he saw the peak of his mountain rising in the distance. European eyes gazed on the "roof" of the Karakoram for the first time.

Twenty-six years later, K2 was revealed in all its glory. Colonel Francis Younghusband, on his way from Kashgar in the Sinkiang Region to Srinagar, traversed the Old Muztag Pass from North to South. During the climb he was presented with the breathtaking sight of K2. Younghusband was later to write "It seemed to emerge like a perfect cone, incredibly high. I was astounded."

The presence of a traveller-explorer from the Val d'Aosta, Roberto Lerco of Gressoney, at the foot of K2 in 1890 is worthy of mention. After having explored the valleys around Nanga Parbat, Lerco and his group of Balti porters pushed on up to the first slopes of K2's South-East Ridge, which eventually took the name of Abruzzi Ridge. This was an exploit ahead of its time, but one that is recorded only in Lerco's oral accounts (which are, however, full of precise geographical details).

In the summer of 1892 William Martin Conway, a noted London art critic, writer and explorer, penetrated the Karakoram Range at the head of a small expedition. He was accompanied by Major Charles Bruce, four Gurkhas, Oscar Eckenstein (famous for having invented modern crampons), the Alpine guide Matthias Zurbriggen from Macugnaga in Italy, the painter McCormik and two other Englishmen, Colonel Lloyd Dickin and Heywood Roudebush. In July the group explored the Biafo and Hispar glaciers. In contrast with his companions, Eckenstein used avant-garde technical aids: an ice axe with a handle just 85 centimetres long, and ten-point crampons — a minor revolution. In August, near the confluence of the Upper Baltoro and Godwin Austen Glaciers, the group came within sight of K2. The great ice plateau reminded Conway of Place de la Concorde in Paris, hence was christened Concordia. There

was, however, no question of making an attempt on the summit of K2. The conservative Conway and the young Eckenstein proved incompatible travelling companions, to the extent that the latter abandoned the expedition as they came off the Biafo Glacier. Conway was not to be denied a personal triumph, however. Together with Bruce, Zurbriggen and two Gurkhas he climbed to 6,890 metres on the Golden Throne, setting an important new height record. The expedition returned to London to great public acclaim. Conway and his companions had coloured in one of the empty spaces on the world map and

34 top *Henry Haversham Godwin Austen, an officer in the service of the Survey of India, was the first Westerner to look upon the summit pyramid of K2.*

34 bottom *The Londoner William Martin Conway, an art critic, writer and explorer, led an expedition to the Karakoram in 1892. He was accompanied by Charles Bruce, four Gurkhas, Oscar Eckenstein, Matthias Zurbriggen, the painter McCormik, Lloyd Dickin and Heywood Roudebush. In August, close to the confluence of the Upper Baltoro and Godwin Austen Glaciers, they came within sight of K2.*

had provided the impetus for the creation of a new popular myth. The K2 odyssey originated here. After an interval of ten years, the new century was greeted by a serious attempt at climbing K2.

The moving spirit behind the first true mountaineering expedition to K2 was the indefatigable Eckenstein, who led a curiously mixed bunch of climbers. The group included the expert Austrian climbers Victor Wessely and Heinrich Pfannl, the Swiss doctor Jules Jacot-Guillarmot, and George Knowles, an art collector. The most controversial member of the team was, however, none other than the Irishman Aleister Crowley, irreverent, bizarre iconoclast, wizard and poet, heroin addict and pornographer, coprophiliac, animal lover and chess player. In the course of his life Crowley was to call himself Master Thérion, Count Vladimir Svareff, Laird of Boleskin and Abertarff, Sir Alaster de Kerval, Prince Chioa Khan, Frater Perdurabo and the Great Beast 666. He was convinced that he was the reincarnation of Cagliostro, the occultist Eliphas Levi and Pope Alexander VI Borgia. Fifty years after the death of the Irishman, the historian Walt Unsworth described him as a charlatan and dabbler in black magic and sacrilegious arts, in the *Encyclopaedia of Mountaineering*. At the end of the nineteenth century, however, Crowley was also an excellent climber and first class mountaineer. He had important solo climbs including many of the classic peaks of the Western Alps, a number of "firsts" and long high-altitude traverses to his name.

The 1902 expedition was not lacking in drama. Early on, the members of the expedition arrived at the base camp without their leader Eckenstein, who was arrested on the Kashmir border (it has been suggested that Conway, recently elected President of the Alpine Club, had something to do with this episode) and not released until three weeks later. Some time later, an exchange of opinions over the route to follow to the summit developed into a full scale row. Crowley wanted to attack the South-East Ridge while the others decided to head for the North-East Crest.

The Irishman was proved right as the group was forced to turn back at 6,000 metres. In a fit of rage on the crest, Crowley reached the point of threatening Knowles with a revolver. A struggle followed and Crowley was disarmed. The ascent of K2 having failed, the group decided to aim for the saddle between K2 and Skyang Kangri (7,544 metres, the Staircase). However, at 6,200 metres Pfannl was struck by pulmonary edema. Only Crowley, despite his ignorance of medical matters, realised the gravity of the situation and insisted on taking his companion off the mountain. This time the others listened and the descent saved the Austrian climber.

35 *A bizzare, irreverent iconoclast devoted to the occult, the Irishman Aleister Crowley was undoubtedly the most controversial member of the Eckenstein expedition to K2. However, he was an excellent climber and experienced in high mountains.*

38 *The Duke of the Abruzzi, with his guides and a number of porters, leaving on an initial reconnaissance trip around K2.*

39 *From the Savoia Glacier, K2 presented an inaccessible face of gigantic proportions. But it was not from this side that the Duke's expedition was to attempt to climb the Karakoram's highest peak.*

highest point that had ever been trodden by human foot."

In the following years it appeared from one moment to the next that a new expedition was due to depart in the direction of K2. In fact none of them did, as the available resources were insufficient for enterprises on this scale. The first to return, and then to the eastern Karakoram, were the scientists. Filippo De Filippi, a medical biologist who had been with the Duke's 1909 expedition, succeeded in putting together, in 1913, an extremely well qualified scientific team that included many of the most well known figures among the academics of the era. The geographical and geological aspects, for example, were entrusted to Giotto Dainelli and Olinto Marinelli. The entire group, supposed to pass through the Himalayas, the Karakoram and Chinese Turkestan, was in Srinagar by mid-September. They took 35 days to reach Skardu, much longer than the Duke, but this was only to be expected as the trek was slowed down by numerous scientific surveys and observations. During the autumn and winter, Dainelli, the Alpine guide Joseph Petigax and a number of porters left the main party and headed for the Baltoro. In mid-February 1914, following a three and a half-month stop at Skardu, the De Filippi caravan proceeded on towards Ladakh, the second stage of the expedition prior to arriving in Chinese Turkestan.

In 1927, on the eve of the tenth anniversary of victory in the Great War, the climbers returned to the charge. The time was ripe for new projects and the epic Everest adventure had begun in the Himalayas. There was talk in Milan of organising an expedition to K2 in 1928. The funds would apparently be provided by the City of Milan, and the sponsoring bodies would be the Italian Geographical Society and the Milan section of the Alpine Club.

A leader already existed, Giotto Dainelli, which meant that the expedition would have both scientific and climbing objectives. However, during the preparatory phase Dainelli unexpectedly withdrew and the whole project had to be reorganised. Dainelli's place was taken by Aimone di Savoia, the Duke of Spoleto, but as so much time had been lost it was decided to

postpone the expedition to the following year, and to send only an advance party to the Karakoram in the summer of '28. In the meantime, the Transarctic expedition led by General Nobile, with the dirigible *Italia*, ended in tragedy.

The political world was shaken by endless disputes and it was felt that another failure would discredit the regime in Italy. The situation worsened. In the end the expedition was revised and given a scientific and exploratory rather than mountaineering bias.

Under the direction of the Duke of Spoleto, the group left for the Karakoram on the 18th of

42 *The imposing pyramid of K2 is peerless. From the Southern Crest of the Staircase, the Duke of the Abruzzi's camera captured the might of the glacial masses covering the Eastern Flank.*
Photograph by Duke of the Abruzzi.

43 *It was clear from the earliest reconnaissance made by the Duke and his guides that the "conquest" of K2 should be attempted via the South-East Spur.*

camp alone. Wiessner refused to give up and tried to climb again but understandably he failed to get beyond camp II. No trace was ever found of Dudley Wolfe, his tent or his rescuers. They were probably all buried by an avalanche.

A few months later Europe was shivering under the winds of war and the Karakoram closed in on itself once again. Climbers eventually returned to the area in 1953. Great changes had taken place in the shadows of the great mountains in the intervening years. In 1947 Pakistan was created as an independent Muslim republic. The new state included the entire Karakoram Range and its eight-thousand-metre peaks. The access route to K2 now followed a different direction. Srinagar was now out of bounds as it was located in the Kashmir region controlled by India. As an alternative, a rudimentary airstrip allowed an air link with Rawalpindi, weather conditions permitting of course. American voices were heard in Skardu once again early in June, 1953, and some of the Balti may have recognised familiar faces. Among the climbers were Charles Houston and Bob Bates, two veterans of the '38 expedition. Their six companions were young, skilled and daring climbers, but they had yet to experience really high altitudes.

The expedition aroused great expectations. Just a few days earlier the Himalayas had been shaken by the incredible news that Edmund Hillary and Sherpa Tenzing Norgay had succeeded in becoming the first men to tread the 8,848-metre summit of Mount Everest. In the euphoric climate of those days it was all too easy to predict a similar conquest of K2. Dreams usually turn out differently when confronted with reality, and this was to be no exception. Thanks to the experience and knowledge of the Abruzzi Ridge garnered fifteen years earlier, the Americans climbed rapidly. Without encountering any problems, they staked out the route to the Shoulder before the conditions worsened. For days the mountain was literally besieged by bad weather. The climbers stuck it out in their tents at camp VIII at an altitude of 7,700 metres, but the wind and snow refused them a moment's respite. Houston's and George Bell's tent was ripped to shreds by the gales and the two mountaineers only

just managed to squeeze under the canvas shared by Bates and Tony Streather. It was a difficult few days, and the situation turned critical when Art Gilkey fell ill. Houston, a doctor, diagnosed thrombophlebitis. They had to get off the mountain, even if it meant dragging the patient across icy slopes. In apocalyptic conditions and fearing the worst, the group moved off. They were exhausted by the time spent at high altitude and the extra fatigue of carrying Gilkey had them stumbling. The retreat towards camp VII was made even more dangerous by the risk of avalanches. It was decided to lower Gilkey vertically, avoiding the dangerous traverses. Things were going well when Bell, descending behind his companions heading towards Gilkey, slipped and fell headlong. His fall dragged down Houston, Bates, Dee Molenaar and Gilkey in a tangle of ropes. Bob Craig, who had already reached camp VII, watched the scene helplessly. Everything occurred in a few short seconds, and just as catastrophe seemed inevitable the miracle happened. Pete Schoening, who had just lowered Gilkey from above, felt a terrible wrench. The rope came close to breaking, friction burned his gloves and hands but his belay held and was enough to slow and eventually halt the fall.

The consequences were serious, but could have been much, much worse. Houston appeared to have suffered most with a violent blow to the head. In one way or another, however, the climbers all managed to make it to camp VII. All, that is, except for Gilkey who was left anchored to the slope by two ice-picks, waiting for room to be made in one of the tents. With a suitable refuge arranged for their companion, the strongest climbers ventured out once again. They were faced with an 80-90-metre traverse, but Gilkey had literally disappeared without trace. A snowslide? The following day, descending towards camp VI, the climbers came across a few bits of cloth, nothing more. The descent to the base camp was interminable. Bell had frozen feet and the others were faring no better. Completely unexpectedly, help arrived from below. The Hunza porters, by now resigned to descending without the group, intercepted the climbers just above camp II.

"We set off again along the glacier dominated by colossal ruined castles of granite with walls 2000 metres high. Towards midday we reached Concordia... It appeared suddenly before us as a dreamlike vision as we came out of a depression in the moraine.

At Concordia we left the Baltoro to reach the Godwin Austen Glacier along a spur of snow emerging from the moraine. We marched for hours along the white trail flanked by the pale ranks of ice spires resembling the sails of a regatta. Towards evening we reached the foot of the Southern Wall of K2 where the deep valley of the Godwin Austen deviates to the East as it receives the Savoia Glacier. We pitched camp at around 5,000 metres alongside the site which formed the base camp for the Houston expedition and where we came across a few pieces of unusable equipment lying on the ice. The program for the following day included a reconnaissance trip up to the Saddle of the Winds should the sky be clear, or to the start of the main crest of K2 if not. When we left the tent at around dawn, the blizzard clouds covered the two masses. The fine spell of the previous days had broken and so we adopted the lesser program...

We had already achieved our principal reconnaissance aim."

Ardito Desio,
"Rivista Mensile
del Cai", 1954

FRITZ WIESSNER

KURT DIEMBERGER

*I*n 1939, on the upper slopes of K2, Fritz Wiessner was a whisker away from writing a unique page in the history of Himalayan climbing, but held back out of consideration for his companion, Sherpa Pasang Dawa Lama. Having reached a point 200 metres from the summit late in the evening, Pasang was consumed by fear of the gods and demons which would have woken at nightfall. "Sahib, no, tomorrow!" he pleaded, and nothing in the world could have convinced him to proceed, not even the knowledge that the summit of K2 was just 200 metres of easy climbing away. The two had, in fact, already overcome the last difficult rocky spur which, in any case, was no serious obstacle to the US-resident, but Dresden-born mountaineer Weissner.

"Pasang was inflexible in his decision," Fritz told me during a conference tour I made in his adopted country. "I was tempted to cut loose, and climb alone. But I'd never done anything similar before. Anyway, the weather appeared settled, and I was sure I'd have another chance so I decided to turn back."

Had Fritz Wiessner not made this decision, he would have been the first man to have set foot atop an 8,000-metre peak, eleven years before Maurice Herzog and Louis Lachenal on Annapurna.

He would, moreover, have climbed the world's second highest mountain without the use of oxygen, a feat forty years ahead of its time. This leaves aside, of course, George Mallory and Sandy Irvine's attempt on Everest in 1924, but in their case no one will ever know whether the two British climbers reached the summit before disappearing.

How did things turn out on K2 in 1939? During the descent, the crampons tied to Pasang's rucksack worked loose and were lost.

As Schiller wrote, "What you may be offered in a moment all eternity will never give you back." Neither Fritz Wiessner nor Pasang returned to that point at 8,382 metres. The summit was barred to them, and what was so nearly a triumph ultimately turned into a tragedy, the first to strike K2, in which four men lost their lives.

47 A thoroughbred climber and extremely experienced mountaineer, Fritz Wiessner might well have reached the summit of K2 in 1939 had he enjoyed a modicum of good fortune. Together with Sherpa Pasang Dawa Lama, he reached 8,380 metres without the use of oxygen.

THE YEAR
OF THE CONQUEST

Photographs by Archive Centre, National Mountain Museum, Turin

48 *On the occasion of the conquest of the world's second highest mountain, the Italian Post Office decided to commemorate the event with a series of stamps, but following the controversy after the expedition's return, they were withdrawn.*

49 top *Before beginning the approach march to K2, the climbers posed for a souvenir photo. From the left, kneeling, Gino Soldà, Lino Lacedelli, Guido Pagani, the expedition doctor, Erich Abram and Walter Bonatti. In the centre row, from the left: Mario Pùchoz, Cirillo Floreanini, Sergio Viotto; in the centre, Ardito Desio. Top, from the left: Achille Compagnoni, Ugo Angelino, Ubaldo Rey, Pino Gallotti, Bruno Zanettin, one of the four scientists and Mario Fantin.*

ollowing a gruelling return trek, the final curtain drew on the Houston expedition at Skardu. The American climbers were in poor condition and their morale had been shattered. In those difficult days, however, other climbers were looking towards K2 with hope and optimism. Professor Ardito Desio and Riccardo Cassin were in Pakistan by the end of August. Desio had obtained authorisation for a trip in the "area adjacent to the Baltoro." and the two made a decisive advance on the slopes of K2.

In reality, this was actually a reconnaissance trip: for some time plans had been in discussion for a new, all-Italian expedition to the Karakoram giant. The project could have come to fruition as early as the summer of 1954, but authorisation from the Pakistani government had not yet been obtained. No word had been received from Karachi regarding the application made by Desio early in January (the second, following a request made in the summer of 1952). As always in these cases, the silence inspired no confidence in the eventual outcome, but given the personal support of the Alcide De Gasperi and that of the Italian foreign office for the mountaineering expedition, it was inexplicable. Before boarding the plane for Skardu, Desio and Cassin had just enough time to meet the survivors of the recent expedition to K2 at the Rawalpindi home of the Pakistani colonel Atta Ullah. It is hard to imagine that they did not gain precious information on the ascent routes.

The first phase of the journey into the mountains of the Karakoram involved a lengthy diversion. The government had asked Professor Desio for the benefit of his geological expertise: the entire Stak Valley in Baltistan was threatened by a glacier which in just three months had advanced no less than 12 kilometres, an average speed of over 110 metres a day. Fortunately, the extraordinary and frightening phenomenon appeared to have passed through its acute stage. Ardito Desio realised that the uncontrollable flow of ice had come to a halt, and informed the government authorities that the danger had passed, and that the inhabitants of the villages could sleep soundly once again.

On the 19th of September a small caravan left the haven of Askole in the direction of K2. At the head of the column, the two Italian sahibs were

untiring. Desio knew the area well: twenty-four years earlier he had explored at length in the high valleys and glaciers of the region in the company of the Duke of Spoleto. Since then he had scaled the heights of the scientific and academic world, but without interrupting his travels. Since 1922 he had carried out research in Asia Minor, Albania, various African regions and the mountains of Persia, as well as in the Karakoram. In all he had been involved in around a dozen expeditions. For his part, Riccardo Cassin was still one of the leading figures in Italian mountaineering. Compared with the years of his extraordinary feats in the Dolomites and on Mont Blanc, he was more mature, perhaps even less impulsive, but his strength was still the stuff of legends and his experience incomparable.

At midday on the 25th of March, the caravan reached Concordia. The immense bulk of K2 rose before their eyes. Some months later Desio confided to the readers of the "Rivista Mensile del Cai" that "It appeared almost unexpectedly as in a dream (...). It stood against the sky like a colossal granite monument lightly draped by the ermine of its glaciers, placed by nature as a challenge to the furies of the wind and the ambitions of men." From the same vantage point, in the spring of '29, K2 had so impressed the Italian geologist as to leave him with "an indelible memory, full of desires and intentions." Perhaps the idea of an Italian attempt on the highest peak in the Karakoram Range was conceived at that moment. The fact remains that just ten years later, Professor Desio had already outlined a project. His estimate of the expedition expenses contained a significant innovation: the use of air transport to take the men and equipment to the base camp. After sounding out opinions at the Alpine Club, it appeared that the project was certain to progress into the execution phase.

The party's departure for the Karakoram appeared imminent, but the outbreak of the Second World War put all plans on hold. Desio was not one to give up easily, however, and in 1946 he picked up the traces. He dusted off his old project, updated it, contacted the Italian air force and even wrote to a number of American helicopter manufacturers. The idea of air transport was, however, too far ahead of its times and the expedition had to rely on more traditional means.

49 bottom *Ardito Desio,
Professor of Geology at the
University of Milan, and
leader of the 1954 Italian
expedition, had already
participated in 12
scientific expeditions to
various parts of the world
when he left for K2.*

A sudden snowfall on the glacier slowed the group's progress, and the return of the fine weather complicated matters still further. The glare was blinding and there were not enough sunglasses for the whole group. The ranks of the Balti were struck by ophthalmia and many wanted to turn back. The enterprise came very close to failure. Eventually, following lengthy negotiations, some of the porters continued, although many loads were abandoned en route. On the evening of the 13th of May, the caravan reached Concordia. The panorama with K2 dominating the skyline was fabulous, but there was no time for celebrations. The Balti were exhausted and had reached breaking point. The base camp was only five hours march away, but their proximity to the objective understandably left them completely indifferent. With the exception of eight Hunza high-altitude porters, the other bearers made their way home. Desio thus turned to the Pakistani officials attached to the expedition: they would have

to turn back and recruit more men at Askole.

The next day, the small surviving group identified a suitable site for the base camp. For the moment, however, only one tent was pitched on the site. Something of a disaster had struck the expedition. Things did not improve until the 19th of May when, together with the climbers still at Askole, new squads of fresh porters arrived. More groups of Balti arrived over the following few days, the abandoned loads were recovered and all the equipment was eventually brought up to the 5,000-metre high base camp. It was not until the 31st of May, however, that all of the material and men had reached the foot of K2. There was not a minute to spare, and the Abruzzi Ridge had to be attacked immediately. The first climbers to reach the base camp had actually already begun to pitch the lower camps on the Abruzzi Ridge.

On the 29th of May, Compagnoni and Rey pushed on as far as camp III, at 6,308 metres. More tents had to be added, however, and above all the loads had to be hoisted to the higher altitudes. Between the first two camps the team used a winch which had been brought from Italy, and constructed a similar device at the base camp. The climbers and porters worked non-stop until the 4th of June, but then bad weather slowed their rhythm. On the 14th, Compagnoni reached 6,500 metres at the foot of the challenging House's Chimney. Two days later camp IV was established beneath the rocky wall. As the group climbed, the route was equipped with fixed ropes, a precaution which allowed the climbers to return to the camps safely, even in blizzard conditions with zero visibility.

The expedition appeared to be progressing well, but without anybody realising it, things suddenly took a turn for the worse, a prelude to a tragedy. On the 16th of June, Mario Pùchoz reported an irritating sore throat. He must have been sweating when he reached one of the high-altitude camps and then got caught in the chill winds. However, the Alpine guide from the Val d'Aosta was not one to complain. His fortitude and stamina were legendary, and a slight cough was not going to stop him from climbing. Nevertheless, three days later he had still not recovered; anything but. In the meantime the weather had worsened. On the 20th of June, at camp II, Pùchoz began

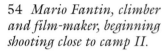

54 *Mario Fantin, climber and film-maker, beginning shooting close to camp II.*

55 top *Once the tents had been pitched at the 6,095-metre camp II, they provided an excellent outpost from which to reach the high camps along the Abruzzi Ridge.*

breathing irregularly, a sign that something was seriously wrong. On being informed of his companion's condition, Guido Pagani, the expedition's doctor, immediately climbed up from camp I. At first the guide's health did not appear to give particular cause for concern, but the following day his condition deteriorated. The diagnosis was bronchopneumonia. He needed to be taken down into the valley as soon as possible but the weather conditions were prohibitive. Pagani never left the patient and used the oxygen cylinders to help him, administering what medication he had to hand. There was nothing more that he could do. Mario Pùchoz died at one o'clock at night on the 21st of June. With the benefit of hindsight it is easy to diagnose an acute pulmonary edema, but in that era relatively little was known of the terrible effects of high altitudes. The bad weather continued for some days, and it was not until the 26th of June that Pùchoz's body could be recovered. His companions buried him next to the tombstone erected by the Americans the previous year in honour of Art Gilkey. The future of the expedition momentarily appeared to be in doubt. The team's morale had hit rock bottom, and there were few who wanted to proceed at all costs. Things only gradually returned to normal as the climb ahead began once again to occupy the thoughts of the small community encamped on the lower slopes of K2.

As soon as the weather improved, House's Chimney was climbed and ropes were installed. The second winch was located on the brow of the rockband, and proved indispensable for hauling the heavy loads up to the newly established camp V. Two days later Abram and Gallotti equipped the ascent route up to the site of camp VI with fixed ropes; at this point the altimeter read 7,300 metres. Over the following days tents, supplies and

equipment were brought up. Life was more difficult this far up as the high altitude began to make itself felt. On the 18th of July, Compagnoni, Rey, Lacedelli and Bonatti pushed on as far as the Shoulder of K2, the terrace which housed the Americans' eighth high-altitude camp (and where the Italians pitched their seventh). The summit was now beginning to draw nearer. The provisioning of the higher camps required the climbers and the small group of Hunza porters, unmatched high-altitude workers, to perform back-breaking labours in alternating fine and foul weather. Only Abram, Bonatti, Lacedelli, Gallotti, Compagnoni, Floreanini and Rey remained fit and ready at high altitude.

On the 28th of July, at 7,700 metres, camp VIII was pitched just below a great wall of ice.

55 bottom *The climbers on the Italian expedition brought the body of Mario Pùchoz, the victim of acute mountain sickness between the 20th and 21st of June, down to base camp.*

We were still on the Baltoro Glacier, in the area known as Urdukas, where we stayed for several days to acclimatise to the altitude, and it was there that I was the victim of a stupid incident for which I nearly paid dearly. It happened like this. One morning as a joke Lacedelli entered my tent to wake me up and grabbed me by the arms, me and the sleeping bag in which I was wrapped up. Imprudently he dragged me over the threshold of the tent and began rocking me. But suddenly I slipped from his grasp, out of the sleeping bag and began rolling down the icy slope as naked as the day I was born.

It was what you might well define as a "heavy" joke. I garnered cuts and bruises which kept me out of action for around ten days. When I came to, stretched out on the floor of the large supply tent, Lacedelli was standing there with a face like a caned dog. However, so as not to create problems for him with the strict expedition leader, I agreed with those present that my forced convalescence should be put down to a "stomach bug." For the record I should point out that my "sickness," faked so as to protect my companion, soon back-fired on me as it was a sign of physical weakness in the eyes of those who were unaware of the truth. Worse was to come when the K2 story was told later and I was attributed with non-existent illnesses for that epsiode. Once again, as would appear to be the rule, an altruistic gesture was repaid by the ingratitude of those who knew the truth and had directly benefited.

Walter Bonatti,
"Il caso K2",
Ferrari Grafiche

56 top *Cirillo Floreanini taking on a load at camp III to be taken up to the next camp.*

56 bottom *Lino Lacedelli setting up some fixed ropes on the Abruzzi Ridge. In the background you can see the confluence of the Godwin Austen and Baltoro Glaciers.*

Compagnoni and Lacedelli occupied the tent, as the following day they were due to climb and establish a higher camp, the last one prior to the final push to the summit. The worst appeared to be over, but on the 29th of July the climb suffered a severe set-back. The leading team was forced back by the difficult going, and the pitching of the minuscule camp IX was postponed until the following day. The supply lines were also suffering from problems, however. That evening at camp VIII, the general meeting point, only Bonatti and Gallotti arrived with a tent, two respirators and

some food. There was no oxygen as it had been abandoned by Abram and Rey, who had turned back. Plans were made for the following day, and it was decided that Compagnoni and Lacedelli would attempt to pitch camp IX, while Bonatti and Gallotti would descend to recover the oxygen gear.

Up until this point the story has followed a single plot, but subsequent events were to be recounted in two different ways. As we shall see, the differences were substantial. We begin with the official version, as recorded in the account of the expedition. The following morning, having descended to recover the oxygen gear, Bonatti and Gallotti met Abram in the company of two Hunzas who had reached him the previous evening close to camp VII. All five climbed together, dividing the loads among them. However, the first defections came at camp VIII: Gallotti and the Hunza Isakhan were exhausted and stopped, while the others pushed on.

Higher up, Abram also surrendered to exhaustion, and only Walter Bonatti and the porter Mahdi proceeded towards camp IX with the oxygen. "But when night fell," wrote Ardito Desio in the "Rivista Mensile del Cai" in 1954, "they were still on the march. However, they nevertheless succeeded in identifying camp IX and attracting the attention of their companions. The two climbers in the higher camp shouted down to Bonatti and the porter to leave the loads and descend to camp VIII as there was a dangerous snow-covered wall above them that was impossible to negotiate in the dark. Mahdi was in no condition to climb higher anyway, and asked to turn back. The two decided not to risk a descent, however, preferring to dig a hole in the snow in which to spend the night and to head down the mountain at first light."

In a piece they wrote for the book "La Conquista del K2" (*The K2 Conquest*), the official account of the expedition edited by Ardito Desio, Compagnoni and Lacedelli went into more detail: "At dusk we heard shouts. We immediately left the tent. Bonatti and Mahdi were not to be seen because it was already dark, but we could hear their voices. Unfortunately communication was extremely difficult as the wind whipped away our words." Lacedelli finally had the impression that Bonatti was calling to say that he could make it up

on his own, but that Mahdi wanted to descend. "'Go back,' we shouted, 'Turn back.' We never imagined that the two would have decided to spend the night at that altitude with neither a tent nor a bivouac bag. As Bonatti's voice was no longer to be heard, we thought that he had already turned back." After a sleepless night, Compagnoni and Lacedelli left their tent at dawn. Above them the sky was clear, but below there was nothing but a sea of clouds: "(...) We tried to spot the oxygen respirators that Bonatti and Mahdi must have left. 'Look, there's someone descending.' Was it Bonatti or Mahdi? At that distance it was impossible to tell. We called, the figure stopped and turned but did not reply. He then started stumbling down the precipitous slope again. 'What's happened?' we asked ourselves. We ran through all the possible hypotheses without striking upon the one that had actually occurred. We could hardly believe that two men could have survived an entire night at 8,000 metres with no shelter from the cold and the wind."

This was how Achille Compagnoni and Lino Lacedelli described the events in the "Rivista Mensile del Cai" in 1954: Having descended to recover the oxygen gear, the two camp IX climbers recall beginning climbing at a quarter past six. The ascent over soft snow was slow and exhausting. Higher up, the channel crossed directly by Wiessner in 1939 proved impracticable due to the masses of unstable snow. There was no way through the rocks to the left. After various attempts, the pair began to climb immediately to the left of the channel. Compagnoni fell, but Lacedelli succeeded in negotiating the passage. Shortly afterwards a rocky stretch was also successfully climbed, but there was still much snow to be covered. Following another difficult passage, the first oxygen tank registered

empty. The pair proceeded cautiously; at this point mistakes could prove fatal. A complicated traverse across a rocky turret followed. Compagnoni and Lacedelli remembered being left without oxygen at around four o'clock: "... A horrible sensation. We were breathless and an oppressive sensation of heat affected our heads and feet, our legs were weaker and it was difficult to remain standing... It was then that we realised that the oxygen was finished." ("Rivista Mensile del Cai", 1954).

But there was still ground to be covered. With an enormous effort of will, the two climbers decided to continue. Gritting their teeth, they proceeded without even dumping the empty tanks. It was too steep, too dangerous, they were to say later. The summit was still some distance away and the last stretch appeared unending. Close to the peak, the wind blew the clouds away and suddenly the horizon expanded, revealing a fantastic panorama across the mountains of the Karakoram: hundreds of snowy peaks of every shape stretching as far as the eye could see. A dreamlike world. The climbers' torment ended at six o'clock in the evening. They described the summit of K2 as like "a great icy ridge, slightly sloping towards the North. It could comfortably accommodate a hundred people." Three thousand six hundred metres below them, in the "chasm of the Godwin Austen Glacier," they could make out the base camp. An embrace, the ritual photos and a few shots with the cine-camera for the eventual film, with fingers numb with cold, and then half an hour later it was time to head downwards. It was a difficult, risky descent in the dark with dangerous slips and two terrifying falls, fortunately with no serious consequences. It was a quarter to midnight by the time Compagnoni and Lacedelli reached camp VIII, where their companions were waiting.

We mentioned earlier that there are two versions of this story. Some years after the conclusion of the expedition, Walter Bonatti recounted the events of the team's last few days on K2 rather differently than the expedition leader and the summit team. This was in 1961: in a chapter of "Le Mie Montagne" (*My Mountains*), a cult book for an entire generation of climbers, the young Lombard mountaineer (Bonatti was 24 at the time of the climb) described in detail the events which preceded the conquest of the summit. On the evening of the 29th of July 1954, he wrote, a precise plan of action was drawn up in the tent at camp VIII.

Compagnoni and Lacedelli were recovering from the attempt to pitch camp IX; Bonatti and Gallotti had succeeded in climbing that far but the oxygen gear had been left lower down. The only solution was another attempt to recover it. According to the agreed plan, the following day Compagnoni and Lacedelli were to pitch the tent for the final camp 100 metres lower than originally planned, so as to alleviate the fatigue of their companions who would be bringing up the oxygen. This plan would have had Bonatti and Gallotti coping with a 200-metre descent and a 500-metre climb. With the oxygen gear on their backs (each set weighed nearly 19 kilograms) it was a Herculean task, but one which had to be completed if the leading team was to have any real hope of reaching the summit.

On the morning of the 30th of July, during the final stages of the descent, the two climbers responsible for the recovery of the oxygen met a fit-again Erich Abram, Isakhan and Mahdi. It was a welcome surprise, as the presence of reinforcements could only increase the chances of the established plan succeeding. Things went smoothly as far as camp VIII, where the exhausted Gallotti and Isakhan were forced to call a halt. After resting, Abram, Bonatti and Mahdi set off again at half past three. An hour later they were already beyond the great wall of ice dominating the penultimate camp. They even succeeded in exchanging a few words with their companions above: "Lino! Achille! Where are you? Where have you pitched the tent?" "Follow the tracks." The voice which replied from above did not appear to be far away, but the camp was anything but close at hand. Could Bonatti and Abram have taken the wrong route? There was no option but to continue, even though the difference in height to be covered was far greater with respect to the previous evening's agreements. At half past six, Abram surrendered and turned back. Bonatti and Mahdi proceeded alone. They thought that their companions' tent may have been pitched below the suspended serac. But there was no trace of Compagnoni and Lacedelli in that area. It was clear that the camp could only be some way off line, considerably farther to the left,

below the rockband. What were they to do?

It was now late, but they made a last push before darkness fell. There was still no sign of the camp. Bonatti's torch had given up the ghost with the cold, and Mahdi was getting nervous at the idea of spending the night at that altitude. He suddenly began to shout and appeared to be losing control. There was no reply to his calls and the situation was fast becoming critical. The slope was steep, the altimeter read well over 8,000 metres and there was no chance of descending in the dark as it was far too dangerous. Bonatti had no choice but to

58 Mario Fantin in high altitude gear is immortalised by the camera while himself struggling with photographic equipment. Born in 1921 at Bologna, Fantin was attached to the expedition with the task of shooting film sequences.

59 Guido Pagani and Ugo Angelino climbing towards camp III along the line of fixed ropes.

AN ENDURING CHALLENGE
FROM THE FIRST REPEAT CLIMBS TO SPEED CLIMBING

62 *The upper section of the South-South-West Ridge and the West Face are still bathed in the sun, but just a little farther on the clouds have already obscured the Southern Side of K2.*
Photograph by Galen Rowell/ Mountain Light

T he "conquest" of K2 had an enormous impact and not only in mountaineering circles. For months the Italian newspapers dedicated long articles to the enterprise and its background. The identity of the two climbers who had reached the summit was not revealed until the autumn, in accordance with an unwritten agreement reached by the members of the expedition.

Of course, reporters and paparazzi were on the rampage for weeks in search of scoops and fresh pictures. This frenzied hunt for news inevitably led to a number of false scents being taken up.

A newsreel company of the era, claiming some form of divinatory power, named Compagnoni and Rey as the conquerors. In the end it was Professor Desio who revealed the secret. In the meantime, however, celebrations were underway at Genoa and Milan. In March of 1955, the climbers and scientists of the expedition were received by Pope Pius XII in the Vatican, and then by the President of the Republic, Luigi Einaudi, at the Quirinale. In the same period cinemas throughout Italy were showing the film "Italia K2" (no less than 53 copies were distributed) by the director Marcello Baldi.

It was an interesting effort and a great popular success. The usual talk of football was put aside in favour of K2, and the names of all the climbers were familiar to the man in the street.

An incredible patriotic fervour surrounded the enterprise. "They've won! The best news for

the Italians for many years," wrote Dino Buzzati in the "Corriere della Sera." It should be pointed out that this was a delicate moment in Italian history: the country was in the middle of post-war reconstruction and although the economy was beginning to recover, there were still plenty of problems waiting to be tackled. Emigration was a flourishing phenomenon and a large part of the population lived in impoverished conditions, so much so that just two years earlier a parliamentary inquiry had revealed the presence of 12 million "poor" and "underprivileged" people. In a situation of this nature, social tensions reached dangerous levels very quickly. Only great sporting events, invariably used as a means to national solidarity, succeeded in restoring calm during these difficult post-war years. The mechanism functioned admirably in 1948, at the time of the assassination attempt on

Palmiro Togliatti, when Gino Bartali's victory in the Tour de France contributed to defusing the threat of civil war.

The first ascent of K2 was no exception to the rule and had international as well as national repercussions. The "conquest" of the Karakoram giant was promoted as the ragamuffin Italy's triumph over the world superpowers. Terms such as honour, glory, homeland, sacrifice and conquest made their reappearance after the dark, harsh years of the war.

It is true, however, that even abroad the news of the K2 climb had created a stir. The major European climbing magazines dedicated ample space to the event: after all, following the conquest of Everest in 1953, another of the great Himalayan myths had been disproved, that of the inaccessibility of the earth's second highest mountain.

62-63 A realm of ice, great serac falls and snow-filled channels created by the avalanches, the Southern Face of K2 rises between the South-South-West Ridge, to the left in this photo, and the Abruzzi Ridge.
Photograph by Gary Ball/Hedgehog House

THE SECOND ASCENT

Photographs by Galen Rowell/Mountain Light

G iven this climate, one might legitimately have expected a steady flow of new expeditions to the Karakoram. Things turned out rather differently however. It was not that the peaks of the region were ignored by the climbing community — quite the reverse — but that the Fifties saw a burst of interest in other objectives such as Broad Peak, Chogolisa and the Gasherbrums. Another attempt on K2 was not to take place until 1960. In the spring of that year, a mixed expedition composed of American and German climbers attempted a repeat of the Abruzzi Ridge climb. Led by Major W. D. Hackett, the group included the Germans Wolfgang Deubzer, Ludwig Greissl, Günther Jahr and Herbert Wünsche, and the Americans Davis Bohn and Lynn Pease. The group was forced to turn back at 7,260 metres by the terrible weather.

Following this attempt K2 and the surrounding mountains were effectively barred to the international mountaineering community for fifteen years. Between 1961 and 1974 the war between India and Pakistan kept the climbers away. The Baltoro Muztag region — which included all the 8,000-metre peaks in the Karakoram Range — was only reopened to mountaineering expeditions in the mid-Seventies. The Americans returned to K2 in 1975. The expedition was led by Jim Whitaker (the first American to reach the summit of Everest, in 1963) and the climbing team comprised Galen Rowell, Fred Stanley, Leif Norman Patterson, Fred B. Dunham, Robert Schaller, Jr., Lou Whitaker, Jim Wickwire and Dianne Roberts (wife of Jim Whitaker). Things looked promising, but once again the Americans were dogged by ill-fortune: bad weather and a strike by the porters forced the climbers to turn back after reaching no higher than 6,700 metres.

A year later it was the turn of the Poles, a team composed of experienced climbers, albeit unknown outside their own frontiers. The expedition was led by Janusz Kurzab and aimed at the North East Ridge, the route attempted by Oscar Eckenstein's team in 1902. Having overcome all the major difficulties concentrated in the central section of the route, the climbers pushed on much higher. On the 12th of August, 1976, camp VI was pitched at 7,900 metres. The leading team was to

64 top *The majestic beauty of the Southern Face of K2 dominates Concordia.*

64 bottom *The climbers on the 1975 Whitaker expedition allow themselves a moment's rest in the tent at the base camp.*

65 *In the Concordia area, at the confluence of the Baltoro and the Godwin Austen Glaciers, a line of porters slowly approaches the K2 base camp.*

66-67 *A climber on the 1975 American expedition climbing the snow-covered slopes below the Savoia Saddle.*

68 left *Three climbers from the American expedition ascending the first part of the North-West Ridge with heavy packs.*

68 right *Jim Whittaker struggling with fixed ropes in a previously equipped passage. In that year the American climbers reached only 6,700 metres.*

69 *Rob Schaller closing in on the Savoia Saddle. At his shoulder the panorama has extended into infinity.*

On May 25, 1975, with 330 porters, we reached Concordia. The long-awaited view of K2 was suddenly before us.

The base of the great peak lay hidden in rolling clouds while a white plume blew from its summit. The bulk and perfect symmetry of the mountain filled the valley of the Godwin Austen Glacier as a diamond completes a fine setting.

We had all expected that coming suddenly face to face with K2 at a distance of only 10 kilometres would be a soul-stirring experience. To the contrary -- the mountain was everything we expected it to be, and nothing more. No pulses quickened; no tears flowed. Ecstasy, if anyone felt it, was well contained. Long days spent battling porters and each other had sapped our emotional energy. After six hard weeks of travel, we were just nearing the beginning of our task.

The summit of K2 looked cold, remote, and distant. Anyway, as I stood at Concordia, I felt the strong presence of those who had been there before me.

The sight of this major peak brought Himalayan history to life.

Galen Rowell,
"In The Throne Room of the Mountain Gods,"
Sierra Club Books

depart from this point. Two days later, Leszek Cichy and Jan Holnickiszule attempted a blitz, but they were forced back just below a rockband at 8,200 metres. The following morning a reserve team comprising Eugeniusz Chrobak and Wojciek Wroz made a do-or-die bid for the summit. They eventually made it to 8,400 metres, but the summit was some way off and the weather conditions were not encouraging. Moreover, there was a lot of unstable fresh snow, the difficult passages reached grade V and the oxygen supplies were running short. At six o'clock in the evening, after a rapid conference, Chrobak and Wroz turned back. It was unfortunate because they deserved much more for their efforts.

The spring of '77 saw some new faces in the Baltoro region. The arrival of a large Japanese expedition threw the high Karakoram villages into confusion. In just a few hours hundreds of Balti porters and a robust platoon of Hunzas were recruited (the reports of the time talked of a total of 1500 men!): the supplies and equipment belonging to the Japanese team were of a considerable weight and bulk. The 41 climbers from the Land of the Rising Sun were led by Ichiro Yoshizawa. He had devised a plan of attack in grand style: the climbers were to be employed in roll-over shifts along the route, the length of the Abruzzi Ridge was to be equipped with fixed ropes and oxygen was to be used at high altitudes. Together with the climbers, the group of high altitude porters were to continually supply the six high camps along the ascent route. Moreover, links were to be maintained with the base camp via both radios and messengers. Following furious toing-and-froing which lasted for some weeks, the first climbers reached the summit at ten to seven on the evening of the 8th of August. Tsuneo Shigehiro, Takeyoshi Takatsuka and Shoji Nakamura were then obliged to bivouac at an extremely high altitude because of the dark. The news of the conquest was relayed via walkie-talkie to the base camp 3,600 metres below.

The next day the summit was also trodden by Mitsuo Hirishima, Masahide Onodera and Hideo Yamamato. The 33-year-old Hunza porter Ashraf Aman was also part of this group and was the first Pakistani to touch the roof of the Karakoram.

THE DEATH OF
NICK ESTCOURT

*Photographs by
Chris Bonington*

*I*n the spring of the following year, a British expedition quietly approached the South-West Ridge (or West Ridge as some improperly continue to call it) of K2. This was a small group composed of a team of renowned, highly experienced climbers, the crème de la crème of British Himalayan mountaineering: Chris Bonington, Peter Boardman, Paul Braithwaite, Jim Duff (the doctor), Nick Estcourt, Tony Riley, Doug Scott and Joe Tasker. In contrast with the

The only trace of the avalanche was the cone of snow at the bottom of the hanging glacier, but that had been there before. It didn't seem any bigger, yet thousands of tons of snow and ice must have poured down, sweeping Nick with them. There were just a few puffy afternoon clouds in the sky, not a breath of wind, everything was

tranquil under the hot afternoon sun. Back in camp the survivors, Doug Scott, Peter Boardman, Joe Tasker, Jim Duff and I, were grappling with the grief, shock, guilt, and relief at still being alive, trying to come to terms with what had happened. It was the end of an era. Nick had been one of my closest friends and a loyal support on Annapurna, Everest and now K2.

Chris Bonington,
*"Mountaineer"
Diadem/Hodder &
Stoughton, 1989*

Japanese attempt, the British expedition carried a minimum of equipment and engaged a limited number of porters. This was not a budgetary question, but rather a policy decision representing the complete antithesis of the spirit behind the Himalayan enterprises of the preceding years.
It is true that some of the climbers mentioned took part in the great national expeditions to Annapurna and Everest, but times had changed and it was time to change with them. It was only right and proper that even the highest mountains were to be climbed without undue recourse to the wonders of modern technology and on restricted budgets. In other words, "light," clean expeditions were the order of the day, even in the Karakoram and the Himalayas. As far as the 1978 British expedition is concerned, it would technically be wrong to talk about a true "Alpine style," but

70 At the base of the South-West Ridge space for the camp was at a premium, but there was sufficient to pitch a few tents.

70-71 Peter Boardman climbing determinedly towards camp II. This was a very dangerous passage: on the 12th of July, 1978, Nick Estcourt was swept away by an avalanche here and died.

71 bottom Nick Estcourt (left), his face burned by the sun, resting in the tent at camp I alongside Joe Tasker.

72 This shot shows the avalanche which killed Nick Estcourt on the 12th of July, 1978. After two days of heavy snow falls, fine weather had returned and the skilled British climber was climbing to the 6,500-metre camp II. Doug Scott and a Hunza porter who were following Estcourt at a certain distance were spared by the gigantic mass of snow.

At about midday, when I was resting at Camp I with Jim Duff, a huge avalanche poured over the ice cliffs to our right. With a reflex action I started to take photographs, until Jim shouted, "For God's sake stop! Nick and Doug could be in that." They had set out from the camp about two hours earlier to ferry loads to Camp II. We tried to convince ourselves that the avalanche would have missed them, but about an hour later Doug rushed into the camp with news of Nick's death. Our expedition had ended in tragedy at its very beginning.

Chris Bonington,
"The Everest Years,"
Hodder & Stoughton,
1986

compared with the traditional methods — a systematic assault on one face, ridge or rib — it is undeniable that a transformation was in progress. Bonington and company intended to trace a new route, benefiting from the help of the porters only to a certain altitude and to cover as much of the climb as possible without oxygen.

Beyond the base camp, pitched on the Savoia Glacier at 5,400 metres, things proceeded smoothly up to 6,700 metres; here the bad weather struck. The group was forced to retreat. However, after two days of heavy snowfalls, the skies cleared and the 12th of June was a beautiful day. Doug Scott, Nick Estcourt and a Hunza porter were climbing towards camp II at 6,500 metres. In order to reach their destination they had to cross a broad slope. The snow appeared to be holding, but as a safety measure the two climbers proceeded at a distance of around 100 metres one from the other, equipping the route with a light fixed rope to facilitate the transportation of the successive loads. Behind them followed the Hunza Kamajan. Scott was almost in

sight of camp II when he heard a violent crash. Behind him the entire slope was moving: 200 metres higher up a huge avalanche had started. The mass of snow overwhelmed Estcourt, hurling him down the mountain. In spite of being out of the direct line, Scott was pulled into the snowslide by the line linking him to his companion. That he survived was a miracle due to the heavy, bulky load he was carrying on his back. It was rooted deep into the snow and anchored him to the slope.

A few hundred metres lower down, at camp I, Bonington and Duff were unaware of the tragedy: they had seen the avalanche, and one of them had photographed the distant spectacle. Only later were they to learn the truth. It goes without saying that the expedition was immediately suspended.

72-73 *At the base of the South-West Ridge one can clearly see where the avalanche broke away.*

THE AMERICAN ROUTE

*Photographs by
John Roskelley*

*I*n that same year, a few months after the derailed British attempt, K2 was climbed for the third time. The honours went to an American expedition, the sixth to take to the slopes of K2 since 1938. The new group, led by the veteran Jim Whittaker — the very same Whittaker of '75 — was composed of Craig Anderson, Terry and Cherie Bech, Chris Chandler (who had reached the summit of Everest in 1976), Skip Edmunds, Diana Jagersky, Louis Reichardt, Rick Ridgeway, John Roskelley, Robert Schaller, William Sumner, James Wickwire and Dianne Roberts.

The climbers reached the foot of K2 late in the season, at the beginning of July, as the Pakistani authorities had refused them permission to bring their schedule forwards. With the base camp installed, the teams attacked the North-East Ridge attempted by the Poles two years earlier. Five high-altitude camps were pitched, the last at 7,700 metres. Then came the last push, the race to the summit. The final part of the route resisted the assault, however. The only option open to the Americans was to improvise. While Roskelley and Ridgeway made a last attempt on the Ridge, Wickwire, Terry Bech and Reichardt crossed the East wall and reached the Abruzzi Ridge. On the 5th of September they pitched a tent a little below the ridge at 7,850 metres. On the 6th of September, Reichardt and Wickwire left for the summit from this camp. They took with them just two oxygen cylinders, insufficient for a full ascent and descent, but they were hoping to use the masks and respirators only on the last part of the climb. Wickwire strapped on his mask just above 8,000 metres. Reichardt pushed on without oxygen for some time, but when he tried to use his cylinder higher up he found that the supply tube was fractured. Reichardt decided to attempt the climb anyway, dumped his load and proceeded.

The two climbers reached the summit at twenty past five in the afternoon, after 13 hours of gruelling effort. Wickwire lingered on the summit, reluctant to miss an opportunity of exposing a few rolls of film, and told his friend to descend. Reichardt needed no second bidding: there was only an hour and a half left before nightfall and he was worried. He descended as fast as he could

74 *The slope is covered with deep snow, but the fixed ropes are a considerable aid to progress. Led by Jim Whittaker, in 1978 the Americans climbed the North-East Ridge as far as 7,700 metres and then continued along the Abruzzi Ridge to the summit.*

75 *Rick Ridgeway, here tackling the gruelling task of ferrying supplies to the high camps, reached the summit of K2 on the 7th of September, 1978, together with John Roskelley. Even though they carried cylinders up to high altitudes, the team completed the climb without using oxygen.*

Our team's struggle to climb K2's North-East Ridge in 1978 had taken over 60 days above base camp. Jet-stream winds, deep snow, team strife, and route difficulties had kept us from taking the last step to the summit. The five of us still able and willing to go for the top reached Camp V. There were two distinct routes to the summit: the direct finish up the still unclimbed North-East Ridge, or a long traverse to the Abruzzi Ridge. Rick Ridgeway and I believed we should finish the North-East Ridge, first pioneered by the Polish in 1977, but left incomplete. Our team-mates, Lou Reichardt, Jim Wickwire, and Terry Bech, decided to attempt the Abruzzi Ridge finish. While they fought deep snow to traverse the slopes to the Abruzzi, Rick and I made little progress up our intended route. Continual winds from the Southwest had loaded the slopes with waist-deep snow, making them dangerously prone to avalanche. Defeated after three days on our route, we turned our efforts to the Abruzzi, where, according to reports on our two-way radio, Reichardt and Wickwire were finding the slopes free of deep snow and easily ascended. Bech had descended because of illness. We descended to our team-mates' tracks of the previous day, and we listened to the excitement at base camp over the radio as Lou and Jim reached the summit late in the evening. But, excitement soon turned to worry, as night blackened the slopes and only Reichardt returned to camp just before midnight. Wickwire had bivouacked below the summit. At two o' clock, under cloudless skies, no wind, K2 finally felt our footsteps.

John Roskelley

while taking all due precautions. The last section was complicated; there was not even a hint of a moon in the sky and it was pitch black. Suddenly he saw a light: it was Roskelley and Ridgeway who, having abandoned their attempt on the North-East Ridge, and after having reached the minuscule camp on the Abruzzi Ridge, were waiting for their friends. Reichardt entered the tent at half past eight.

Higher up the mountain, Wickwire was already preparing to spend the night: 150 metres below the summit he realised that he would not be able to reach his companion, dug a hole in the snow and crawled in with his bivouac bag. It was very cold and the oxygen bottle had been exhausted some time before, but the shelter was sufficient to protect him from frostbite.

At three o'clock in the morning, Roskelley and Ridgeway made their attack on the summit. At 8,320 metres they dumped the oxygen bottles, which up to that point they hadn't used, and climbed to meet Wickwire. He was on his way down and did not appear to have suffered unduly. He was sure that he would make it down on his own, saluted his friends and continued on his way.

The pair climbed well, with Roskelley leading. They came through the trial without any particular physical problems, but they recounted having experienced hallucinations during the last stretch. They reached the summit by half past one. This was the first time that a climbing team had reached the top of K2 without the aid of oxygen. It could, of course, be argued that they had brought oxygen bottles with them up to very high altitudes and that they thus had a safety net in case of trouble. But it was nevertheless quite a feat.

In that very period, the use of oxygen at extremely high altitudes was the subject of intense debate. In the spring, Reinhold Messner and Peter Habeler had succeeded in climbing Everest without oxygen, demonstrating that man can approach the 9,000-metre mark with no serious damage to the organism. The news aroused great public interest, and the medical community was not slow in putting forward its opinion. The most authoritative voices claimed that in theory only climbers of extraordinary physique can do

without breathing gear. The lead climbers of the Whittaker expedition, on the other hand, held contrasting opinions. When interviewed on the subject by the UK magazine "Mountain," Rick Ridgeway provided a very surprising reply: "I've never considered myself to be any kind of superman or even super-athlete. I can only run a few miles and 20 push-ups knock me out. I'm at my best drinking beer, smoking dope and hanging out rather than spending time in boring training...".

78 *A short distance from the tents, Rick Ridgeway climbs along the crest; it is not difficult but one must concentrate.*

79 *The 7th of September, 1978, Rick Ridgeway poses for the ritual photo on the summit of K2.*

MESSNER'S ASCENT AND THE FRENCH ATTEMPT

Photographs by Archive Alessandro Gogna/K3

The fourth successful ascent of K2 came in the spring of 1979. The expedition was led by Reinhold Messner, already a famous figure throughout the world. The Sudtirolese climber could boast an exceptional record: in eight years he had climbed four eight-thousand-metre peaks (Manaslu, Hidden Peak, Everest without oxygen, and Nanga Parbat, of which he completed the first traverse in 1970 and the first ascent without oxygen in 1978), quite a feat. His companions were extremely skilled climbers: the German Michl Dacher, the Austrian Robert Schauer and the Italians Alessandro Gogna, Friedl Mutschlechner and Renato Casarotto. The latter had recently stunned the climbing world with a series of exceptional feats including first ascents of the North Face of Huascaran in Peru, and the North-East Tower of Fitz Roy in Patagonia. Messner's scheme was nothing if not ambitious: he planned to open up a new route — the Magic Line — which, starting from the Negrotto Saddle, should have followed much of the South-South-West Ridge of K2. This plan was not put into practice, however. Once he had reached the area, the expedition leader decided to forego the Ridge and to fall back on the classic 1954 route. With just three high-altitude camps, a single bivouac, fixed ropes only on the most exposed sections, and without oxygen, Messner and Dacher reached the summit on the 12th of July.

Around the same time, the South-South-West Ridge of K2 was the subject of the insistent interest of a large French national expedition led by Bernard Mellet. The climbing team was composed of Yannick Seigneur, Maurice Barrard, Pierre Beghin, Jean-Marc Boivin, Dominique Chaix, Patrick Cordier, Jean Coudray, Xavier Fargeas, Marc Galy, Yvan Ghiradini, Thierry Leroy, Dominique Marchal, Daniel Monaci and Jean-Claude Mosca.

To this group one also has to add film and television cameramen. Naturally, such a large group had an abundance of materials (around 30 tons of supplies and equipment) as testified by the number of porters engaged — 1400 as far as the base camp.

The caravan established its base camp at the foot of K2 on the 9th of July, and the next day

80 *The gruelling ferrying of the packs along the Abruzzi Ridge route; in the background is Mitre Peak.*

81 *As one climbs the Abruzzi Ridge, the view extends to the great glaciers surrounding K2: the Godwin Austen and the Baltoro.*

Sixteen years on from that glorious summer of 1979, I can think back to what it meant to me to venture onto the steep slopes of K2 and attempt to reach the summit. Although free of tragedy or even close-run incidents, the experience was sufficient, and since then I've never again tried to climb an 8,000-metre peak, even though I've continued to spend my life in the mountains. Having come so close to conquering the summit, my good health and having had excellent companions with whom to try and try again greatly disturbed me.

It didn't last long, however. I soon realised that that was K2 justice. Initially the weather conditions had forced us to spend a night at 8,000 metres, three in a tent, and then beat a retreat the following morning in the midst of a terrible blizzard; then there was my unwillingness to force things. These were the two elements that disturbed me. Something had upset my equilibrium; something had told me to give it up, and so I did. Over the past sixteen years I've never regretted my decision.

Personal equilibrium is a vital weapon for a climber; perhaps it is not sufficient but certainly necessary. Alterations to your personal equilibrium may come about involuntarily, but when they do you should take note and act accordingly. K2 may be the symbol of a failure (felt as such and therefore painful), or the symbol of a transformation, of growth, of the awareness of having followed a false trail. It is up to us to decide; and afterwards to smile.

Alessandro Gogna

camp I was already being pitched at 5,600 metres. The tents of the next camp were pitched at the Negrotto Saddle, the snowy depression between the Angelus and the South-South-West Ridge of K2. Camp III was pitched at 6,950 metres on the 20th of July, but then bad weather forced the group to retreat for a week.

As soon as conditions improved the climbers and high altitude porters recommenced equipping the route and supplying the camps. Unfortunately, one of the Hunza porters was the victim of an accident on the route up to camp IV. The climb was difficult and tested the climbers to the limit. Beyond the ice-cap, three further camps were pitched at 7,500, 8,000 and 8,350 metres. Early in September repeated attempts to reach the summit were made in vain, reaching little higher than the last tents. The weather had taken a decided turn for the worse and a withdrawl was unavoidable.

83 *bottom Back from the summit of K2, tired but happy, on the 12th of July, 1979, Reinhold Messner (left) and Michl Dacher allow themselves a brief rest.*

I returned to the West Ridge with Pete Boardman, Joe Tasker and Dick Renshaw in 1980. This time we opted for a technique somewhere between the Himalayan and Alpine styles which we nicknamed the "modular technique." What it boiled down to was this: we would use a thousand metres of fixed ropes to supply camp I, then recover the ropes and repeat the same procedure from camp I upwards. This formula has the advantage of eliminating direct contact with base camp, whilst still allowing sufficient reserves of fuel and supplies to be carried up so as to be able to see out bad weather even at high altitudes.

But there is a disadvantage: every operation becomes extremely tiresome and slow... Various problems cropped up. Pete and Joe began to compete among themselves, and Joe appeared to resent my role as the older and more experienced climber...

I debated for days, but in the end decided it was better that I should abandon the attempt.

We split up with no hard feelings: in these conditions it would have been imprudent to insist on continuing.

The others left for an attempt on the Abruzzi Ridge which proved rather more dramatic than expected. As for the West Ridge, it was climbed the following year in Himalayan style by a Japanese expedition.

Doug Scott,
"Himalayan Climber,"
Diadem Books

radio from the base camp to order them to turn back. Yamashita, in a worse state than the other two, decided to stop but his companions proceeded. Ohtani and Nazir Sabir reached the summit at half past eleven. An hour later the group was reunited, and by late evening had met up with the support team.

In the same season a Franco-German group led by Yannick Seigneur attempted to open a new route on the South Face, to the left of the Abruzzi Ridge, but was forced back before they reached the Shoulder.

Year by year, the number of expeditions to K2 increased. In the summer of '82 a Polish team led by Janusz Kurczab set its sights on the North-West Ridge. The climbers pitched four high-

86-87 Doug Scott, one of the best known British Himalayan climbers, ascending the South-West Ridge beyond camp I. Photograph by Joe Tasker/Chris Bonington

87 Joe Tasker, with a bulky load of ropes, climbing to equip the route between camp I and camp II on the South-West Ridge. Photograph by Doug Scott/Chris Bonington

altitude camps. At 7,600 metres they crossed the fixed ropes installed by the Japanese tackling the North Spur, but made no use of them: the Polish route continued farther to the right. In the second half of August the weather turned, and an unrelenting wind lashed the crests and slopes of K2. All the Polish attempts on the summit were systematically blocked. On the 5th of September, Eugeniusz Chrobak, Leszek Cichy, Krzysztof Wielicky and Wojciech Wroz pitched their last camp at 8,070 metres. The next day Cichy and Wroz reached 8,230 metres without oxygen.

though a number of bottles were taken up to the high camps for emergency use. This oxygen proved vital on one occasion, at the 6,000-metre-high second camp, when Marco Corte Colò was struck by mountain sickness; without the use of the breathing gear he would not have made it down. He was unable to move his legs and was only semi-conscious. We lowered him by rope all the way to base camp, and the entire expedition's participation in the rescue operation was a moving demonstration of solidarity.

Our team was divided into four groups in order to attack the mountain in rotation. The first group, for example, set off with a load of ropes, ice and rock pitons and so on, and installed the fixed ropes. At times, this last part of the work was left for the following group. Subsequently, the tents, sleeping bags, stoves and rations were brought up to establish suitably spaced camps which would become starting points for the next section of the climb. While two groups worked, the third rested. The system proved to be excellent, even though the continual fresh snow falls created considerable problems for the establishment of camp II at 6,600 metres.

When at last, at the end of June, the camp was ready, another snow storm forced everybody to abandon the tents and the camp was once again wiped out. At this point the morale of the group had reached rock bottom. Fortunately we had plenty of time to make further attempts. At that time the expedition was also hit by an extraordinary accident which, out in the middle of nowhere, with no access to hospitals, put the ability of our doctor to the test.

During this kind of expedition, many climbers claim that the heat produced by just one gas burner is insufficient, and so they often try to use two under the same pan. The system is dangerous — and not only because of the closeness of the two burners — but nevertheless one of our companions, Luca Argentero, a young climber from Courmayeur, decided to adopt and perfect the technique during his turn as cook. He placed two burners inside an empty biscuit tin, hoping to obtain improved shelter from the wind, and then placed his saucepan on top. After a few minutes, however, he began to doubt the worth of his

95 *Up and down from one camp to the next on an unending roller-coaster, with packs stuffed with climbing material and rations: almost all the great K2 routes have been opened up thanks to the laborious establishment of supply lines. Naturally, the higher you go, the harder the work. Photograph by Soro Dorotei*

discovery and took off the pan so as to remove one of the burners. Just as he leaned over, an overheated burner exploded and metal fragments showered the area, hitting him mostly in the face. Fortunately Luca was wearing ice goggles. The lenses shattered but saved his eyes. On the other hand, his nose was rather bent and it took the genius of Doctor Simini to salvage his former good looks. Three weeks were to pass before the patient was allowed to remove his bandages and breathe freely, but he felt so well that he made it to camp III at 7,600 metres.

On more than one occasion Lady Luck proved to be on our side. I was just below the second camp when a rounded chunk of rock broke off above us and fell in my direction. Fortunately, just above me there was a small protuberance; the projectile hit it and whistled passed my ear. I had flattened myself against the rockwall, but Julie had already seen me under the guillotine's blade.

A RACE
AGAINST TIME

Ten years have passed since my trip to Pakistan, but it is as if it had happened yesterday. I left with Alain, Benoît and Dominique, and returned with Jean-François and Stéphane, but without Daniel! On the 3rd of July we reached camp I. Daniel, Stéphane and Jean-François stopped, but I continued with Loretan, Troillet, Morand and Nicole. The snow was

Subsequently — as is only natural— the most popular route continued to be the Abruzzi Ridge. For many climbers the desire to reach the summit of the world's second highest mountain continued to be the principal objective. Exceptions to this rule in the early Eighties were the two ascents of the North Ridge and a Spanish attempt on the South-West Ridge.

An interesting new development was the appearance of "speed climbing." This style of

deep but we reached 7,400 metres and pitched a tent. The others reached us, and we decided to attempt the summit. That evening, at around 8 o'clock, we departed. By 14:00 hours we were at the summit, the sky was clear and the cold wind had died down. Daniel, Jean-François and Stéphane were still at the Shoulder, 600 metres below. Daniel was not to make it down. Fatigue had sapped his strength, and we were also exhausted and we couldn't dedicate ourselves to a search, moreover a strong wind from the North had risen. We waited for him, but then...Our ascent of K2 had been too quick and lacking in incident to talk about.

Eric Escoffier

climbing had been imported from the Alps, and was predominantly a French phenomenon. For some years, especially in the Western Alps, talented young climbers had succeeded in completing ascents in incredibly short times. Climbs that had once required entire days were now blitzed in a matter of hours.

The concept of climbing against the clock soon took hold and caught the attention of the media. The press and television rediscovered climbing and began to hunt down the latest personalities and construct "league tables." In the general euphoria of the time, it appeared that new exploits would topple the entire history of climbing, but certain comparisons only revealed the ignorance of the reporters. You can only climb rapidly along well known routes: the opening up of difficult new routes, over unknown terrain,

requires rather different schedules. In the mid-Eighties the speed climbing sport reached the great Asian mountains. Alongside traditional ascents and "lightweight" expeditions, the first ascents against the clock were made. In the spring of 1984, Krzysztof Wielicki, a 34-year-old Polish climber, succeeded in climbing Broad Peak in a single day. Just a year later it was the turn of K2.

In the summer of 1985, the Frenchman Eric Escoffier climbed to the 8,616-metre summit in two days, taking the classic Abruzzi Ridge route—an extraordinary feat. Immediately afterwards, two of his friends, Stéphane Schaffter and Daniel Lacroix, attempted to repeat his feat. The climb ended in tragedy as Lacroix was killed during the descent. High altitudes are intolerant of errors and weakness even in the era of great sporting exploits.

98 *The 6th of July, 1985:*
Eric Escoffier, in the blue
suit, and Erhard Loretan
posing for their ritual
photo at the summit of K2.
Photograph by Eric
Escoffier Archive

98-99 *Less linear than*
the North Face, the
Pakistani Side of K2 is
more articulated with
spurs, serac bands and
hanging glaciers.
Photograph by
Eric Escoffier

99 bottom
This photograph shows the
key passage on the Abruzzi
Ridge, House's Chimney,
nowadays frequently
equipped with ladders and
fixed ropes. The chimney
was climbed for the first
time by the American Bill
House in 1938.
Photograph by Gregorio
Ariz Martinez

99

They had nothing left to drink. After two bivouacs without a tent they finally reached the ice sheet below the Shoulder of K2, when "suddenly Tadeusz lost a crampon, he tried to grab onto the slope with his ice-pick, but before Jurek could do anything, he lost his second crampon and slipped. He fell into the abyss, colliding heavily with Jurek who only just managed to keep his balance ... The shocked Jurek eventually reached base camp on the 12th of July" (from *K2, The Endless Knot*).

It was as if black magic had bewitched the mountain — a curse which affected even the best of us. A week after the death of Piotrowski, at around seven o'clock in the evening, by chance I looked up towards the Negrotto Saddle. In a gigantic bowl of snow I could clearly see a black speck moving downwards. "Look how quick he is," I said to myself, given that he was at least a couple of kilometres away as the crow flies.

Suddenly the speck vanished: Renato Casarotto had fallen into a crevasse. From the bottom of the chasm, Renato called desperately with the walkie-talkie, pleading with Goretta and me to go to his aid, and quickly; he was in a bad way. Everybody moved at once. We managed to bring Renato up to the surface still alive, but he was already unconscious and a few minutes later died in our arms.

Six climbers had lost their lives on K2 so far that summer — and Julie was very concerned as to the wisdom of trying again. On the 6th of July we had been 350 metres away from the summit. On the other hand, we were perfectly acclimatised and fitter than ever. Was there still a chance for us? And what if one of us reached the top on behalf of the other, so as to settle the matter once and for all? This was what was running through my mind: the idea of a possible solo attempt. Subsequently, better weather was forecasted and many decided to play their last cards. Julie and I were together again. What happened next is not something that can be told in a few words or a couple of pages. Never in my whole life have I experienced anything as terrible as what occurred at 8,000 metres during days

and days of blizzards. Of the seven that set out, and who, after reaching the summit were held prisoner by the elements, only two survived. The others died at the high camp, or just below in a desperate attempt to descend with their remaining strength: my companion, Julie, Alan Rouse, Alfred Imitzer, Hannes Wieser and Mrowka Dobroslawa.

Why did all this happen? (I discussed the reasons at length in my book *K2, The Endless Knot*). During the ascent we lost a vital day; that led us into the deadly trap of a storm which blew uninterrupted for five days. One tent too few in an overcrowded camp had led to the day's delay. At the root of the complex chain reaction which ultimately led to our ruin, was an avalanche which destroyed two high-altitude camps.

Did destiny play a part? The fact that the avalanche spared a single tent, which then became the key element in the tragedy, was undoubtedly due to fate. That K2 is one of the world's most dangerous mountains is also beyond question. And yet I am still troubled by what Peter Habeler said about K2 being a good mountain. Why? What has the mountain to do with the fact that Wojciech Wroz died, hooking himself up at night to a fixed rope which had not been knotted at the end? And yet, a few days later, Mohammed Alì perished on the Abruzzi Ridge due to a rock-fall. But a rock-fall is blind, we are the ones with eyes.

Certainly, the life of a man is in the hands of fate. The laws of nature apply to mountains too. What did Peter Habeler do on Everest? He prayed.

I've been at base camp for two days and the weather, unfortunately, is unchanged: it's still snowing, either during the day or at night, with occasional clear spells of a few hours. The equipment and rations are already at the Negrotto Saddle. Tomorrow if it's not snowing, I'm going to start the climb, hoping to find myself in a favourable position should stable, fine weather arrive. It's about time!

I've "worked" very hard to reach the saddle due to the excess snow. The traces of the French expedition of 1979 on the South-South-West Ridge are for the moment almost non-existent. Just the odd length of rope. And the tents ripped to pieces by the wind at the Negrotto Saddle.

Renato Casarotto

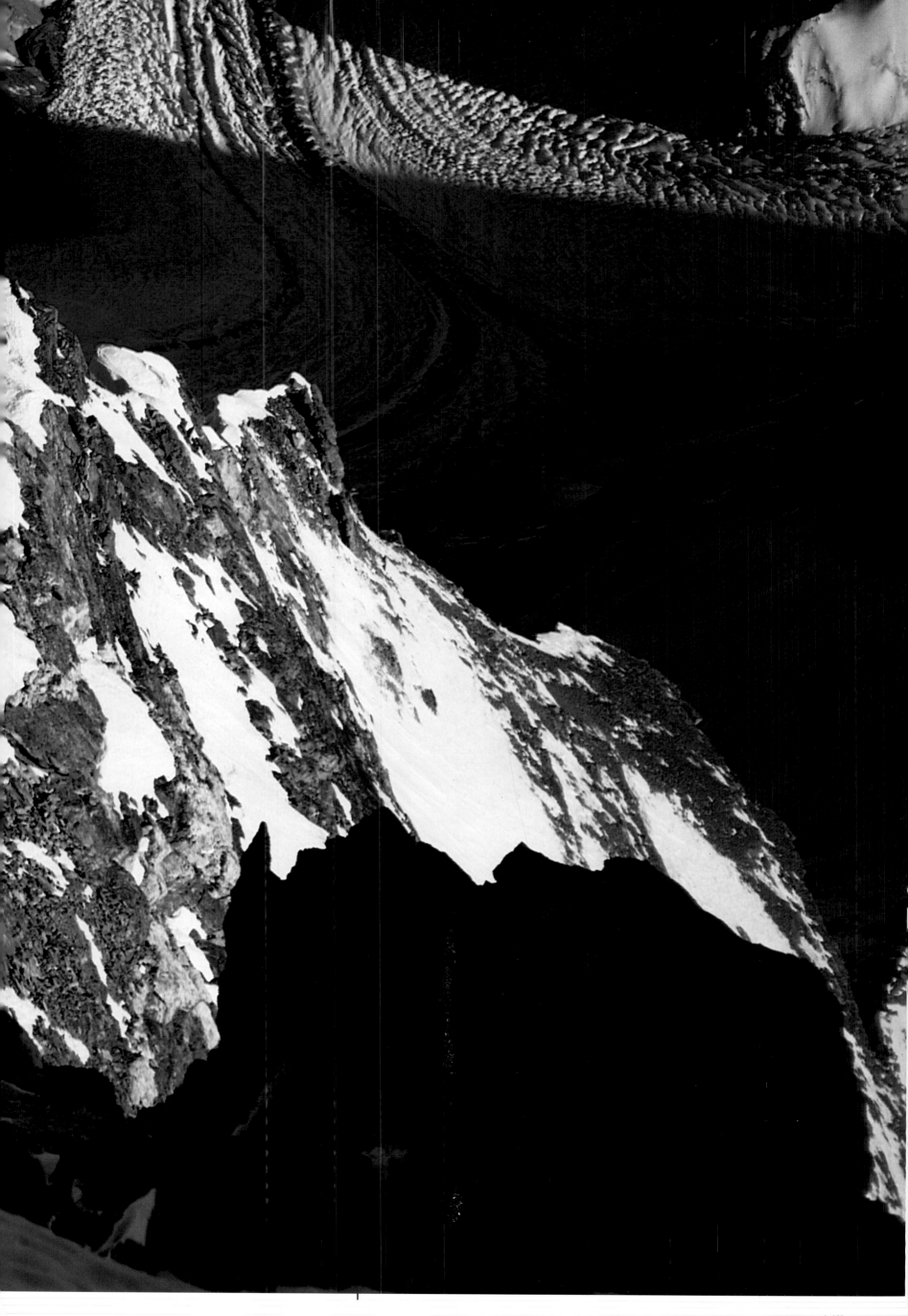

ATTEMPTS, ASCENTS AND A NEW ROUTE

There were also important novelties in 1991, though relatively few expeditions headed to the Karakoram. Among the most notable events in that year's climbing calendar was undoubtedly Pierre Beghin and Christophe Profit's climb along a difficult and complex route. It departed from the Savoia Glacier, followed the North-West Ridge (attempted by the Poles in 1982), crossed the North-West Face in a long, climbing traverse and finished, after having crossed the North Ridge, by following the 1982 Japanese route. Beghin and Profit made a number of attempts, but were frequently beaten by the capricious K2 weather. However, after 45 days of struggle, they reached the summit on the evening of the 15th of August. There was only just enough time for the ritual photo as the sun was setting and the light was poor. They had had to cope with terrible conditions in the upper sections, between 8,000 and 8,500 metres, which had kept them occupied for 12 straight hours. The value of the enterprise lay not so much in the difficulty of the route (Profit declared that he had tackled more demanding passages on the South Wall of Lhotse), but rather the way in which

the two French mountaineers approached the climb. They had no external help (they reached base camp in the company of two friends, doctors not climbers) and a minimum of equipment, and climbed in a true Alpine style. Still in the summer of 1991, there were two unsuccessful attempts on the Abruzzi Ridge, and an Italian attempt on the North-West Face led by Fabio Agostinis that got as far as 8,200 metres up the North Ridge.

The opening to the 1992 season was routine, with three expeditions out of four tackling the Abruzzi Ridge. The objective appeared to be the summit for the summit's sake rather than a search for new routes. The season was marked, above all, by the presence of a large international team led by the Russian Vladimir Balyberdin, well known in the West for the new route traced on the South-West Face of Everest in 1982. His team included another three Russians and two Ukrainians, eleven Americans and one Englishman. The French climber Chantal Mauduit also joined the group, following the retreat of the Swiss expedition led by Peter Schwitter.

The first attempt was made by the Russians. While their companions were holed up at camp III, on the 29th of July Balyberdin and Gennadi Kopieka continued climbing in spite of the wind sweeping across the Abruzzi Ridge. They bivouacked at 7,500 metres. By the 31st of July they had reached the base of the final pyramid at 8,000 metres. They reached the summit at nine o'clock the following evening, without using oxygen, after an 18-hour climb. They were understandably tired, and while Kopieka determinedly headed down, Balyberdin decided to bivouac just below the summit. On the 3rd of August more climbers reached the summit: Chantal Mauduit, solo, at five in the evening and, two hours later, the Ukrainian Aleksei Nikiforov. During the descent Chantal decided to bivouac at 8,400 metres, but when Aleksei reached her, three hours later, the two continued to descend together.

Lastly, following a period of bad weather and the retreat of many of their companions, three Americans, Scott Fischer, Charles Mace and Ed Viesturs, reached the summit on the 16th of August. Two New Zealanders, Rob Hall and Gary Ball, accompanied them as far as the 8,300-metre mark, a little above the passage known as the

130 *Christophe Profit tackling one of the most exposed passages on the new K2 route. Photograph by Pierre Beghin*

131 *Pierre Beghin's camera has lingered on the bivouac tent pitched at 7,950 metres. The photograph was taken at an altitude of around 8,100 metres, and Beghin and Profit have encountered extremely difficult conditions with wind-blown patches and tracts of unstable snow. Photograph by Pierre Beghin*

132-133
*In this photo can be seen
one of the numerous
attempts to climb made
by the Beghin-Profit team.
The two French climbers
arrived at base camp,
on the Pakistani Side,
accompanied by two
doctor friends.
Photograph by
Pierre Beghin*

133 top *At dusk on the
15th of August, 1991,
Christophe Profit could
finally sit in the snow
at the top of K2.
Photograph by
Pierre Beghin*

133 bottom *A moment
later and it's Beghin's
turn for the ritual photo.
Photograph by
Pierre Beghin*

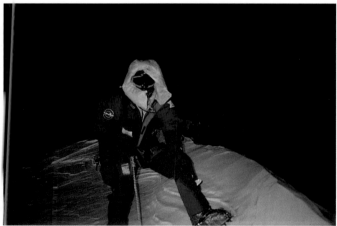

This climb proved to be an interminable succession of stages to be overcome and bottlenecks to be dextrously skirted round. Each step was difficult in its own right. I am convinced that adventure exists only in its globality, and that courage lies in conceiving it. When we find ourselves in the middle of a risky enterprise, all we need to do is lean on reality as if it were a stick and let our instincts guide us.

Within a few months I'll ask myself how on earth I managed in that freezing cold with just the meager comfort of a sip of water and a pinch of salt. I will have crossed a threshold, the threshold of oblivion, the threshold which separates the double life of the adventurer, everyday life from adventure.

Pierre Beghin,
"High Altitudes,"
Editions Didier Richard

Bottleneck. Up until a few days earlier, Rob and Gary had been members of an international expedition led by the Mexican climber Ricardo Torres. This group split up following the death of Adrián Benítez, who fell when a hold gave way not far below the Shoulder of K2. Hall and Ball, however, decided to remain at camp IV. They had already been frustrated once, in 1991, when they were forced to turn back after climbing to 7,600 metres. They left for the summit with oxygen bottles an hour after the Americans, on the 16th of August. Initially the climb went smoothly, but then things started to take a turn for the worse. Gary Ball began to suffer from breathing difficulties. Fortunately the three Americans descended quickly and, after a consultation, the five climbers returned to camp IV together. During the evening the New Zealander's condition worsened. There was only one option: get Ball down to base camp as soon as possible. Thus three days later Ball found himself at the foot of K2, where a rescue helicopter was waiting for him.

In the summer of 1993 there were 11 expeditions. It proved to be another tragic year with no less than five deaths. Two groups were working the North Face of K2 at the same time: a Basque team and an international squad led by Vladimir Balyberdin. The Basques reached 8,000 metres, but the other group turned back at 6,800 metres. Climbers of various nationalities laid siege to the Abruzzi Ridge that summer. It would be impossible to name them all here, but mention of some of them has to be made.

In June, a group led by Tomaz Jamnik and composed of seven Slovenians, a Croatian, a Mexican, a Swede and a Briton attempted the classic route. After pitching four high camps, Carlos Carsolio, Zvonko Pozgaj, Stipe Bozic and Viki Groselj reached the summit on the 13th. Less than two weeks later, the feat was repeated by the Swede, Göran Kropp. In the course of the expedition, the Slovenian Bostjan Kekec was taken ill at camp IV, at a height of 7,860 metres, during an attempt on the summit. His companions gave him what aid they could, but there was nothing to be done. Bostjan died on the 15th of June.

Less than two weeks later, the summit of K2 was gained by an American and two Canadians, Philip Powers, Jim Haberl and Dan Culver, members of the expedition led by Stacey Allison. However, the three climbers reached the top one by one and descended in the same way. Powers was back at camp IV by five o'clock in the afternoon; his companions behind him were following in his footsteps. Suddenly, in the difficult passage known as the Bottleneck, Culver fell and disappeared without trace. It was not to be the last accident that summer.

During the night of the 29th of July, at camp IV, pitched at 8,000 metres, six climbers were turning in their sleeping bags, waiting to depart for the summit. They were members of two separate groups. There were a Swede and a Dane from the expedition led by Magnus Nilsson, and four climbers from Reinmar Joswig's team. The next day, all six reached the summit at different times. The last to make it, when it was already dark, were Rafael Jensen and Daniel Bindner. The descent was dramatic: Peter Mezger disappeared without trace, Joswig slipped and fell into the void, and Bindner, suffering from the symptoms of cerebral edema, lost his balance above the Bottleneck and fell down into the valley. Jensen, who was also in poor condition, was accompanied down to the base camp

by a British group climbing the Abruzzi Ridge.

During the summer of 1993, apart from the other unsuccessful attempts (the Canadian attack on, first, the South-South-West Ridge, and then on the South Face, and an attempted Spanish repeat of the Cesen route), there was also a climb which is well worth describing: the first repeat of the South-West Ridge. The honour went to an international team (four Americans, a Canadian, five Britons and an Irishman) led by the Englishman Jonathan Pratt and the American Daniel Mazur. Various incidents punctuated the climbers' time on the slopes of K2, but the climb concluded positively and with no irreparable damage. Following the installation of five high-altitude camps and 4,000 meters of fixed ropes, Pratt and Mazur bivouacked at 8,200 metres on the 1st of September. They left the next morning at half past six and reached the summit at half past eleven at night on the 2nd of September. They stayed on the summit of K2 for a few seconds before beginning their descent. They finally stopped and bivouacked at 8,550 metres.

THE LAST PROBLEM
A DIRECT ROUTE FROM THE NORTH

KURT DIEMBERGER

Over a period of many years, attempt after attempt was made to reach the summit of K2 from the Chinese side via a direct route running up the North Ridge, including the difficult last 600 metres. In1994, the fortieth anniversary of the first conquest of K2, Don Arturo Bergamaschi, a noted expedition organizer and parish priest from Bologna, hatched an audacious project: a new route across K2's North-West Wall and a climb to the summit for the first time along a direct route.

Apart from Don Bergamaschi, the team comprised Fabio Agostinis, Romano Benet, Sergio Cossinetti (the Tarvisio trio who reached 8,200 metres in 1991), Gianbattista Galbiati, Manuel Lugli, Filippo Sala, Nives Meroi (Benet), and three doctors: Paolo Misini, Leonardo Pagani (the son of Guido Pagani, the medical officer on Desio's 1954 expedition) and Giorgio Zavagli. The Italians were joined by seven Spanish climbers, but that group intended to climb along the Japanese route.

Reaching base camp, the Italian group met an American-British team led by Alan and Adrian Burgess which was tackling the North Ridge. It was no advantage having three expeditions in the area, especially in terms of the use of fixed ropes and the restricted space for high camps. The situation improved when the Italians abandoned the classic route and the Americans retired after having reached 8,100 metres toward the end of July.

Don Arturo's group pitched base camp at 4,950 metres on the 7th of June (35 camels had earlier carried their gear to the snout of the glacier). By the end of July, 1,600 metres of fixed rope had been installed, together with two high-altitude camps (at 5,750 and 6,500 metres), even though avalanches and rock falls frequently forced the team to start over. At 6,200 metres, the Italians' route broke away from the ridge and climbed along the North-West Wall, and from the second camp onwards they installed neither fixed ropes nor permanent camps. At that point all that remained was the final push to the summit.

On the 28th of July, Benet, Meroi, Sala and Galbiati, divided into two teams, climbed Alpine style without oxygen along a ramp set diagonally to the centre of the North-West Wall. They spent the night at 7,300 metres and the day after reached

Forty years on from the first ascent of K2, this is the final page to a long and tortuous chapter in mountaineering history. Undoubtedly there will be more to come. Soon new routes will be traced and conquered, although most of the obvious problems on the gigantic Karakoram peak have by now been solved. There will inevitably be a number of classic repeats and many, perhaps too many, attempts along the usual routes.
At this rate, one can be sure that in a few decades' time, the facts of today will already be archive material.

Roberto Mantovani